Judged

Judged

The Value of Being Misunderstood

By *Ziyad Marar*

Bloomsbury Academic
An imprint of Bloomsbury Publishing Plc

B L O O M S B U R Y
LONDON · OXFORD · NEW YORK · NEW DELHI · SYDNEY

Bloomsbury Academic

An imprint of Bloomsbury Publishing Plc

50 Bedford Square	1385 Broadway
London	New York
WC1B 3DP	NY 10018
UK	USA

www.bloomsbury.com

BLOOMSBURY and the Diana logo are trademarks of Bloomsbury Publishing Plc

First published 2018

British Library Cataloguing-in-Publication Data
A catalogue record for this book is available from the British Library.

ISBN:	HB:	978-1-4742-9833-9
	ePDF:	978-1-4742-9832-2
	eBook:	978-1-4742-9834-6

Library of Congress Cataloging-in-Publication Data
A catalog record for this book is available from the Library of Congress.

Cover design: Irene Martinez Costa
Cover image: Wall after earthquake © FredFroese / Getty Images

Typeset by Integra Software Services Pvt. Ltd.
Printed and bound in Great Britain

For my mother, father, sister and brother
Kathy, Nael, Jayne and Leith Marar
Who came with me, from Beirut to Purley

Contents

Introduction

So, did you judge this book by its cover? Or were you intrigued by the title? The subtitle? And now you encounter these lines are you drawn in or put off by this attempt to engage you directly? It's complicated now I think of it. As I write, I'm conscious of different audiences who might want different things and equally that there is no way to deliver on such a wide range of expectations.

Are you judging me? There is a quick heat in the question which is revealing. Implicit in my tone is chagrin and accusation. 'Don't be so judgemental', I'm saying, in a quite judgemental way. To call someone 'judgemental' always seems like a negative judgement, doesn't it? After all I wouldn't say it after a round of applause, or a compliment. Those more positive appraisals just don't have the same impact. When it comes to judgement, criticism weighs much more heavily than praise.[1]

Calling you 'judgemental' is a defensive move on my part, an accusation that you are being critical and asks you to explain yourself. My question, 'Are you judging me?' is loaded with the discomfort of being scrutinized and found wanting and invites me to judge you in return as a form of protective retaliation. I'm asking what your status is in relation to me and what relevance my actions have to you. 'Who do you think you are anyway?!'

But do I really want you to stop judging me? Sure, right there and then, I do. I want to avoid negative appraisal, so I'd like it to stop. The safer language of 'live and let live', 'each to their own' is where we turn when we feel exposed to the harsh glare, and wish to escape scrutiny.

But true escape from judgement is a fantasy. How can we live meaningfully without being judged at all? Even criticism is necessary to living well. Without it we'd be playing tennis with the net down. Other people are necessary for our survival on many levels. They are sources of pleasure, goods, information, but most of all they shape our self-image and self-esteem. While it can be painful at times, the judgement of others is also a source of significance and a necessary path to feeling justified. A robust sense of self isn't really possible except as reflected in the eyes of those whose views we care about, whether parents, friends, colleagues or other audiences.

Alongside the tribulations and unfairnesses of critical judgement lies the tentative hope for kinder appraisals. Raymond Carver, in the poem 'Late Fragment', written at the end of his life, concluded that he got what he wanted from this life, namely 'To call myself beloved, to feel myself / beloved on the earth.' With Carver we want to feel beloved or at least admired, or respected or just recognized. So, what we really want, but can't ever ask for, is to be judged *well*. And I can't ask for that, because wrapped into that wish is a vulnerable hope that you will not find me wanting *quite independently of that hope*. I don't want your charity, or sympathy, or to turn you into a puppet or to generate mere canned applause. It is hard to admit we want to be judged well, because we need to achieve that happy state without being seen to be seeking it.

The psychoanalyst Leslie Farber[2] describes our attempts at willing what cannot be willed. His examples (I can will knowledge, but not wisdom; going to bed, but not sleeping, eating, but not hunger, meekness, but not humility …) are troubling enough. But this is worse. In the case of receiving good judgement, even if I could will it to happen, the judgement resulting wouldn't be worth having. If there is no attendant risk of receiving bad judgement, then the good judgement we receive loses its value. Judgement worth having needs to be fraught with the possibility of painful failure if it is to matter. And this is why we feel so deeply ambivalent about it, and will often pretend to wish our need for it away. It is really why my question contains emotional heat.

By 'judgement' I'm thinking of the social and moral judgements we make of each other in different forms, mainly evaluations of character or action, including the appearance and status, of another person especially around their competence or motivation. These ways of seeing each other pepper our interactions whether through barely perceptible flinches and gut feels through to more conscious assessments – sometimes negative and sometimes positive, but judging all along. Throughout this book I'll be exploring how this capacity, while necessary, is often partial, inconsistent, self-serving, skewed and for these reasons unevenly distributed. And that this unreliability applies as much to how we judge ourselves as it does to how we judge each other.

The unreliability of our judgements ensures that the understanding we have of each other is similarly limited, which is why no one will ever truly understand you. Much of this book is an exploration of the limits to the knowledge we can have of each other and the corresponding feeling that most of us, for much of the time, can feel unknown, alone and other.

When I was nearly 10 years old, my family moved from Beirut to Purley in south London. We had left after the civil war in Lebanon started in 1975 and headed to be near my mother's parents in Croydon. Our first British summer was the famously hot drought of 1976, with temperatures up in the 30s and people needing to ration water. This at least gave us all, my brother, sister and me, some familiar context in what felt an otherwise very unfamiliar country, a country with people who only had one pair of shorts! We all struggled with the adjustment in various ways, my Jordanian father tackling the idiosyncrasies of 'British middle management' and having to commute to and from the Middle East for work, my mother after fifteen years abroad finding us schools and somewhere to live. The primary school we went to was just up the road from our house in Purley, so an easy commute at least. But it was a disorientating experience nevertheless, not least because the teachers, seeing that I had a Christian middle name, decided to call me Paul, and I didn't have the courage to correct them for over a year.

I remember one afternoon getting the results of a maths test. I had got nine out of ten on the test and should have been pleased with that. Unfortunately, the mark I lost was because I had written the correct answer in Arabic. The answer was six, which written in Arabic is indistinguishable from an English seven. Rather than just let it lie, I decided to mention it to the teacher during the lesson. Too self-conscious to put my hand up, I can remember walking up to the front of the class and leaning over to whisper to him what had happened. He looked at me with disbelief, and clearly thought I was trying to cheat. I felt embarrassed, and falsely accused during my slow walk back to my chair, my ears reddening with shame. I could hear sniggering. The sense of alienation I had in this new terrain was thus underscored, and I gained a painful insight that is expressed well by the writer and psychotherapist Adam Phillips in his book *Monogamy*:

> We work hard to keep certain versions of ourselves in other people's minds; and, of course, the less appealing ones out of their minds. And yet everyone we meet invents us, whether we like it or not. Indeed nothing convinces us more of the existence of other people, of just how different they are from us, than what they can make of what we say to them. Our stories often become unrecognizable as they go from mouth to mouth.

> Being misrepresented is simply being presented with
> a version of ourselves – an invention – that we cannot
> agree with.[3]

My maths test episode stays with me as just one example of
being misunderstood in this way. The story being told of me
was unrecognizable to me. Yet I still internalized enough of the
criticism to judge myself harshly for having made a fuss, and
being foolish enough to get out of my chair. Pathetic! This kind
of vivid example is thankfully relatively rare. But misjudgements,
misunderstandings, misrecognition on a more banal level, are very
common. Slight crossings of wires, mismatches in assumptions,
desires, social missteps, all create a web of miscomprehension
that shadows, and isolates us within, our daily lives. Even when
written in lighter ink, these experiences of misjudgement and
misconstrual, it seems to me, are a central feature of what it is to
be human.

While this is a sobering thought, I'll be arguing later that the
story is not necessarily a bleak one. There is something hopeful
that can come from our misapprehensions. In fact the gaps in
knowledge between you and me often provide creative spaces
in which our protean selves can develop and grow. Too much
knowledge would be claustrophobic, predictable and bland.
As Leonard Cohen puts it in the chorus of his song 'Anthem', a
message echoed in the cover of this book,

> Forget your perfect offering
> There is a crack in everything
> That's how the light gets in.

Judging in the digital age

If you want to see how the terrain of judgement has become more complicated in recent years, just look at how much time and effort we invest in expressing ourselves online. And those who think we have become anti-social with an addiction to screens have got it backwards. As my daughter Anna once reminded me when I complained, 'it is called *social* media, Dad'. In presenting ourselves through digital lenses, only seemingly locked away from everyday life, we are instead locked into networks of others who communicate with and assess each other's presentations of ourselves in a quite intense way. This is not always easy to see. We may focus on connection, relationships and gathering information as we communicate this way but this view tends to require we avert our gaze from how online performances are often set out with the hope we will be assessed well by others, who in turn respond in a similarly deliberate way, creating a hall of mirrors of mutual, hopeful, self-conscious reflections. It is hard to feel good about yourself when you now have a window on to a world of people presenting themselves in their best light, for comparison.

The way self-esteem is fed or starved through this medium can be seen with the rising rates of self-harming and online bullying alongside the everyday flow of selfies, gossip and the growth of tools like Instagram and Snapchat. And, of course, there can be harmful consequences for people who have yet to find out there is no delete button on the internet, who might say and show things they later regret.

Our culture has been so permeated by new forms of communication that we are no longer shocked to hear numbers that would have left us open-mouthed in disbelief a decade ago: two billion people on Facebook consume 500 years of video every day; 350,000 tweets are produced every minute and 650 million blogs are written each day. And all of them adorned with metrics that give you some basis for comparison. You can count how many friends a person has, or how many 'likes' their post receives, their followers and subscribers, their retweets, Tumblr re-posts and YouTube views. And much as we deny the significance of such simplistic measures of success, it is very likely they have some kind of skewing effects on most people's behaviour. When you get out of an Uber you are invited to score the driver by clicking on one of five stars, but you need to remember that they are scoring you too. The first episode of *Black Mirror*, season 3, by Charlie Brooker takes this mutual scoring into a satirical dystopia in which people whose scores are constantly changing and constantly visible to all, panic as their rating falls below 4.2, which then limits their access to high-status goods. Those who have fallen catastrophically to under 2 become the underclass. The power of the programme comes in echoing the ubiquity of digitally mediated social judgement that has so quickly become part of contemporary lives.

Take Twitter. Who can honestly say they have no idea how many followers they have? Who won't feel a little blip of satisfaction to see new followers or re-tweets appearing under that little blue sign dubbed 'notifications'. And who doesn't send out a tweet wondering whether it will get acknowledged in some way? Why tweet at all unless you hope to be noticed and acknowledged? Three hundred and fifty thousand tweets per minute adds up to over half a billion attention-seeking messages every day.

We have all become broadcasters and now can reach much larger audiences with a click of a button than would have been possible for anyone outside of the media industries only a few years ago. And this leaves us open to much faster judgements if we get it wrong. The intensity of judgement is refracted brightly through a digital lens and makes it quite clear that those who thought the internet was a place to express yourself privately got it completely wrong. When Emily Thornberry MP sent out a tweet including an image of a house in Rochester swathed in England flags she was immediately judged harshly for the apparent sneer she was directing at a patriotic working-class voter.

This led to her resigning her post as shadow attorney general within days.

Ill-advised comments made can now race around the world in a Twitter storm as happened to Tim Hunt, the Nobel laureate, whose career was ended within days of making sexist remarks during a conference in Korea.

Jon Ronson's book *So You've Been (Publicly) Shamed* works through many cases of disproportionate punishment meted out to witless Twitterers who have crossed a line. The digital world may have intensified our proneness to judging and being judged in return. But it didn't create that need, it just feeds ancient appetites. Rather like cheap fast food, so ubiquitously available today, that satisfies ancient evolved cravings for sugar and fat, we now can access mechanisms on a scale never seen before that feed the deep yearning we have for giving and receiving social judgement.

I was caught by a simple question recently, from a man who lives in difficult conditions in Zimbabwe. 'Why do people in the West ever commit suicide?' he asked. The question asks how it could be that life could seem unliveable when the profound hardships and deprivations that so many in the world still face have been so abundantly overcome. But we also, despite a culture that encourages us to fill up on luxuries, sense that consumption and material needs met do not ultimately satisfy. This observation also invites us to think about the comparisons we make with others and the standards we are then set by which we might see ourselves as failing. The internal judge of ourselves, based on such comparison, is often the hardest critic we face. In looking at and judging others' lives, we can value our own by those lights, and this can lead to imagining their judgements of us in return. This in turn can lead to internalizing those verdicts, and often to finding ourselves so wanting as to make life seem worth less. Far from the optimistic assumption that our needs become more optional as they move from the primitive basics of food, clothing, shelter and ascend into the more abstract domain of self-esteem and recognition (as Maslow's pyramid[4] suggests), the need to feel justified in our lives, however physically comfortable, is just as profound as the need to thrive on a more basic level.

There is something poignant in Samuel Johnson's observation that 'every man, however hopeless his pretensions may appear to all but himself, has some project by which he hopes to rise to reputation; some art by which he imagines that the notice of the world will be attracted'. It is poignant because we can picture such hope with no guarantee that it will be well met. Or maybe that we picture it will be met with harsh critique or – possibly worse – indifference; the vulnerable hoper is exposed callously to the depleted language of being 'a nobody' instead of 'a somebody', let alone a VIP.

As with economic and other resources, the judgement of others is very unevenly distributed. Some are rich with recognition, applause, goodwill, trust, reputation and others are starved of a good word. This would be bad enough if this uneven spread of good judgement were based on something approaching a fair and rational set of assessments. The courts dispensing 'blind justice' claim to be the emblem, if not the reality, of this ideal. But the worst of it is that the judgements we dispense on a daily basis are flawed in many ways and are unfairly distributed because they are driven by self-serving, hypocritical and skewed perceptions of each other, as I will explore in detail in this book.

This unequal distribution is intimately tied up with other kinds of inequality. Recent newspaper articles have talked about how the middle classes create a glass floor for their children. They have resources to ensure no child of theirs falls below a certain level of attainment and expectation in life no matter their lack of intellectual or other merits, and crucially this is because they have opportunities to increase their confidence in the world: their preparedness to expect to be well judged. As the acutely observant sociologist Erving Goffman commented over fifty years ago:

> [I]n an important sense there is only one complete unblushing
> male in America: a young, married, white, urban, northern,
> heterosexual Protestant father of college education, fully
> employed, of good complexion, weight, and height, and a
> recent record in sports. ... Any male who fails to qualify in
> any of these ways is likely to view himself – during moments
> at least – as unworthy, incomplete, and inferior.[5]

By this account the vast majority of people are stigmatized
one way or another. They have 'spoiled identities' in Goffman's
language. I don't imagine this inequality will change any
more easily than other entrenched unfairnesses that plague
our society, but there may be benefit in exploring the strange
texture of social judgement so as to avoid at least some of those
pitfalls. In this book I want to explore the mechanisms of social
judgement which happen every day so as to better understand
the uncomfortable outcomes we seem to take for granted.
And one of these uncomfortable outcomes is the feeling of
isolation arising from the uneasy sense that people don't truly
understand us.

A tour of this book

When assessing claims it is understandable to ask for the
evidence, and this often means scientific evidence. Evidence
and argument are critically important in supporting claims, and
it is thanks to this scientific principle that we can distinguish
between effective medicines and magic, between bridges that will

carry the weight of traffic versus those that will not. But these are relatively 'tame' problems. The scientific method will not always offer satisfying explanations of more complex phenomena, which are not so tame. By contrast many of our concerns in social life have instead the characteristics of 'wicked problems'. 'Wicked problem' is a term used to describe a problem that does not have right or wrong answers (though hopefully better or worse ones); it is usually so uniquely set in a context that you can't easily generalize from it; and the attempt to identify the dense array of underlying causes changes dramatically depending on what frame of reference you are using.

Many of the major social concerns of our times, such as inequality, good relationships, satisfying work or general well-being fall into the category of 'wicked'. If you want to understand why unhappy families are unhappy in their own way (as Tolstoy said in the opening line of *Anna Karenina*) the sources of evidence and the nature of the argument will be a much wider array than falls within the ambit of experimental science.

And so it is with judgement in my view. Our ambivalent relationship with judgement, our often partial and unreasonable mechanisms for deploying it, and our flawed dreams of escape from that kind of scrutiny certainly can be illuminated by the work of experimental psychology. And I will be drawing on this work throughout the book. But this is also true of the more qualitative insights to be gleaned from philosophy, psychoanalytic traditions, anthropology, sociology, as well as those other deep repositories of human knowledge, popular culture and literature.

To deny this is to resemble the drunk man who leaves a pub one night and goes to the carpark to find his car. On his way, he realizes he has lost his keys. So he goes over to the nearest lamppost to search around for them. A policewoman looking on starts to help him, but after a few minutes of fruitless searching asks whether that's in fact where he lost them and the drunk answers, 'No, I lost them over there', pointing over to an area in the surrounding darkness. The policewoman puzzled asks him, 'Then why are you looking for your keys here, if you lost them over there?', to which the man replies, 'Ah, because this is where the light is good.' It is understandable to look for more certainty than can be had when investigating a phenomenon, and this 'streetlight effect' is a tendency to rely on what is more measurable than what might be more insightful even if harder to explore rigorously. Wicked problems often require that we peer into the dark.

Experimental psychologists nevertheless can help us see some features of human nature that generalize across human experience, and shed light on this by arranging the world to show up these daily illusions. They ask people to imagine a stone being dropped from a plane and then to guess where it would land. By showing the gap between our guesses (straight down) and the reality (miles ahead – we overlook the fact the plane is moving so fast), they can skilfully illuminate the biases and preoccupations that can fuel our outlook on the world. But in looking for such common features it is easy to overlook the very particular experiences that we as individuals encounter every day. An ultra-social animal trades in judgements because reputations are of the highest importance, but the particular experience of such judgement is highly contextualized and unique to the setting in question. To develop some insight into these it is valuable to look to films and novels and other forms of popular culture which tell particular stories set in a particular context. To understand the choices involved in developing a reputation we might turn to the compelling and specific story of Walter White in the hit TV series *Breaking Bad* as much as to generalizable experimental data. As the psychologist Dan McAdams puts it, 'As artists we each fashion a singular, self-affirming life. As scientists, we notice how the life we have fashioned resembles certain other lives; we detect similarities, regularities and trends.' Emphasizing the general over the unique, psychology tends to lump while literature splits.

In the spirit of a multi-level approach I draw on these diverse sources to build a picture that I hope more faithfully reflects the complex, 'wicked' reality, rather than to boil it down merely to what can be determined in the lab. I hope that this diversity of enquiry will also make for a more interesting read and help to justify the judgement you made in picking this book up in the first place.

I start with a tour of the social minefields in which we operate. As we tiptoe our way through convention and expectation, the threat of being judged ill plagues us and exposes us to many forms of social pain. Anxieties about awkwardness, embarrassment and guilt, shame's fellow travellers, police our behaviour in profound ways, leading us to find ways to cope by hiding; by veiling our speech and our behaviour. People vary in the skill and knowledge they can use to develop good enough technique. Most of us move somewhere between seeming cool or chic on the one hand, and awkward and gauche on the other, micro-managing impressions as best we can along the way.

Zoom out from the micro-analysis of impression management and you start to see how reputations rise and fall over time. This is the subject of the next chapter. Reputations are some of the most valuable assets a social animal can accrue. In particular, the best reputations need to manage an unlikely trade-off between being seen as well motivated on the one hand, and as competent or skilled on the other: both moral and able, to put it simply. But no one builds a reputation in isolation. It is granted. Whether you are deemed moral or able, both or neither of these of course lies in the eye of the beholder.

Unfortunately, the beholder's eye is an unreliable one; the subject of Chapter 3. The lessons learned about how we deploy social and moral judgements on each other are sobering. We are laden with implicit biases, moral flinches and yuk reactions, alongside self-serving and hypocritical judgements which are coloured by the group allegiances to which we subscribe. Recent research in social and moral psychology, which I'll explore in this chapter, reveals the scale of these tendencies. Our judgements of each other are far from a fair-minded and neutral assessment, however much we might persuade ourselves to see them in that light.

Understandably, the weight of all this judgement can conjure up fantasies of throwing off the curse of judging and being judged and living independently and authentically. Many share the distaste expressed in La Rochefoucauld's comment that if 'we let our reputation and good name depend on the judgement of other men ... merely in order to make them decide in our favour we imperil our peace of mind and way of life in countless ways'. When we glimpse the unwelcome potency of some of our audiences, whose judgement can be withering, we dream of escape. The iconoclast, the eccentric, the original, all exemplify ideals of freedom from judgement however illusory. On occasion, we look to our animal natures in pursuit of a simpler self-image: think Mowgli or Tarzan. At other times, we look to the originality of artists who complicate their way out of the everyday rush with what looks like true self-determination. These are the escape artists who show us what it might be like to be unencumbered selves, which is the subject of Chapter 4. *The Human Stain* by Philip Roth, with its main character Coleman Silk, provides an extended example of what such a pursuit of freedom might look like, and how fraught the attempt can be.

The final chapter, 'The Last Judgement', is concerned with how our lives are judged in the round. Obituaries and biopics are good examples of how to sum up a life when all is done but not yet said. And yet we know these stories, never quite owned by the person being described, necessarily distort a life in order to make it cohere in some way. A story can reveal and conceal in equal measure. Again, serious literature can offer more subtle insights into the texture of a life and avoid the crudest of distortions and revelations of ordinary story-telling, though without escaping them entirely. There is after all no undistorted view, or neutral ground from which to describe a life as a coherent narrative. Even then the unfairness and unkindness, as well as the sheer complexity and confusion, can persist, guaranteeing that the whole story can never be told; that we will never be truly understood. But a distorted account is better than no account, and is central to feeling that our lives have significance.

It was only as I was finishing this book that I realized it is essentially a counterpoint to my last book, *Intimacy: Understanding the Subtle Power of Human Connection*. As the subtitle of that book suggests, it was an exploration of our need for that elusive sense of knowing someone and being known in return – intimacy as the antidote to isolation. In that book, I argued that we are hungry for that sense of being understood, even if that feeling is elusive, fragile, short-lived and often shadowed by painful shots at that vulnerable hope of connection which fall wide of the mark. This book explores the fact that most of the time we don't experience intimacy. In fact, we operate in a world of imperfect judgements, both giving and receiving them, which we cannot avoid. They are important to us nevertheless. Without them we would struggle to live meaningfully. But they are often biased, self-serving, hypocritical, inattentive or thwarted by the fact of each other's shifting, protean social selves. We may want to be seen, to be recognized, but most of the time that which is seen can only be a partial and often distorted part of the story. Yet it would be wrong to think that the truth lies within, merely waiting to be revealed. We may dance with veils, but it is a mistake to think there is a consistent underlying reality which marks out the true self, or that the clothed one we present to the world is somehow false.

So layered with subtle, contradictory and unconscious preoccupations are we that constant misunderstandings and misrecognitions are not so surprising. It may seem hard to think no one truly understands us, until we realize this is, most of the time, our common fate. We, after all, hardly understand ourselves.

1

The social minefield

My daughter Charlotte surprised me with an answer to a question a couple of years ago. It was the end of the summer holidays, a chance to take stock of things before the start of the new school year. She was answering an annual questionnaire, along with her sisters, which roamed across aspects of their lives to see what had changed from year to year: Who were her friends? What music did she like? What advice would she give to her younger self starting secondary school? Most of the questions elicited familiar-seeming answers, with one exception. In answer to the question 'What superpower would you most like to have?', rather than opting for flying, reading minds or Herculean strength, she said she'd have the power to make awkward situations go away.

I've often wondered at the furtive power of the word 'awkward'. It unconsciously shadows so many encounters even as we downplay its significance. And those who feel more at ease in social settings are still conscious of the threat of awkwardness, because awkwardness is achieved between people. You can't entirely rely on your finely honed social skills to spare your blushes if others aren't in on the act. Do you greet a friendly colleague with a handshake, a kiss (two, three?), a hug? Do you offer someone your seat on the train if you think they are probably (but not definitely) pregnant, or might be feeling old and tired? It doesn't just depend on your own judgement. The smooth interaction we'd like is achieved between people, and not within the control of any individual. It's for this kind of reason that in his book *Interaction Ritual*, Erving Goffman suggested that 'there seems to be no social encounter which cannot become embarrassing to one or more of its participants, giving rise to what is sometimes called an incident or false note'.[1]

Social pain

It seems strange to think it might take a superpower to overcome what seems such a trifling concern. 'Oops, that was a bit awkward' is, on the face of it, hardly a phrase to inspire fear and anxiety. I think of the silly dance I do when approaching a door with a group of colleagues when I've invited them to lunch. What do I do? Do I wait back until everyone else has gone through, even if that means a kerfuffle with the other person in the group who had the same idea, or push ahead so as to hold the door open, at the same time making sure to avoid being patronizing or sexist in our post-chivalric age. What's at stake in getting it wrong?

Nothing much, except the feeling that I might, in a small or subtle way, be judged ill. The premise of this book is that we all care about that very much, even if we are capable of pushing that awkward thought away for most of the time. There are flagrant examples where our sensitivity to judgement becomes visible, which I will come to. But awkwardness has power precisely because it reveals this tendency in more banal, everyday settings. The literary critic James Wood, in a quite different context, comments on how easily some writers can get a character 'up and running' with a single deft phrase. The example he uses is informative and relevant and comes from a Guy de Maupassant story: 'he was a gentleman with red whiskers who always went first through a doorway'.[2] It's telling that this description shows us so much with so little effort. The author is inviting us to make a quick but pretty wholesale judgement of this character. He 'gets him in' using a dozen words or so, and reveals to us as readers how unobtrusively skilful we are in colouring in a character – as good as any satirist. We know what people make of us if we reveal ourselves so carelessly. No wonder I keep going with that tricky footwork even when it would be easier, on so many levels in life, to just walk through the door.

So awkwardness is not as trivial as it seems. It has concealed within it a quite disturbing weight. When you hear that someone 'fell awkwardly' you wince in preparation to hear the damage done. In a social setting awkwardness is the warning sign that things are going wrong, and usually that someone is failing. It sets off an alarm bell. If you are prone to ending up in awkward situations too often you risk being judged as socially awkward in general thereby risking rejection and isolation. As social animals we know that such rejection creates severe forms of social pain, very much akin to physical pain.[3] And in some ways this pain is even worse than physical pain. Contrary to the dismissive shrug expressed in the line 'sticks and stones may break my bones, but words will never hurt me', how often, when asked to remember the most painful experiences in their lives, do people turn first to memories of physical pain?

The social minefield is replete with hazards that might trigger social pain. It is easy to focus on formal laws and rules when explaining how people behave and what they are allowed to do in different settings. But legality and prohibition don't begin to circumscribe and direct our behaviour most of the time. The more fundamental shapers of behaviour come from implicit norms that govern our culture, and these are policed through social judgement. Twitter trolls and social media–inspired gossip are magnified versions of this phenomenon, but outside the digital echo chamber we are alert in daily life to the threat of getting things wrong and exposing ourselves to a critical glare.

It is possible to imagine a world where we break free from judgement, which I will explore in Chapter 4, but it is worth remembering the silent power of audiences that may not make themselves obvious every day but are watching and affecting what we can and can't do nonetheless. The journalist Oliver Burkeman tells in his book *The Antidote* of an exercise he once set himself to confront his fear of embarrassment. He had been reading about the stoics and their oft-proclaimed ability to be indifferent to the judgement of others. So, in pursuit of this level of self-command he decided, while on a packed tube, to announce the name of each station as it arrived, loudly. Surely, he noted, his apprehension flies in the face of logic:

> After all, I know nobody in the carriage personally, so I have nothing to lose from them thinking that I'm crazy. Moreover, I know from past experience on the Underground that when other people start talking out loud to themselves, I ignore them, as does everyone else; this is almost certainly the worst thing that's going to happen to me. And those other people speaking out loud are often talking gibberish whereas I am going to be announcing the names of the stations. You could almost argue that I'm performing a public service.
>
> And so why – as the train begins to slow, almost indetectibly at first, for the approach to Chancery Lane – do I feel as if I want to vomit?[4]

We all have (to varying degrees) what the psychologist Mark Leary calls a 'sociometer',[5] which constantly evaluates whether we are being socially accepted. Our self-esteem for this reason is strongly tied to maintaining high social value, and awkwardness is a sign that this is in decline.

Awkwardness comes in various stripes. Committing the *faux pas* of turning up in the wrong clothes is the standard example of a social error. It is still with us despite the contemporary emphasis we have on informality. In fact, it has become harder to choose what to wear the more informal we have become. The last few weddings I've been to did not quite have an official dress code. And like school children on non-uniform day, the guests ended up thinking harder than they would otherwise have done about what not to wear. In the days running up to each wedding, conspiratorial side-chats abounded as guests checked in with each other beforehand for some comforting synchronization.

A more disturbing thought is that the lack of explicit, coordinated standards of etiquette in such cases can sharpen the sense of exclusion that some might feel. Those 'in the know' can freely express themselves blithe in their unstructured egalitarianism, while those who are not already part of the 'in crowd' have fewer mechanisms or guides to help them participate successfully than they would if the 'rules' were clearer.

But awkwardness doesn't need to be triggered by a gaffe or blunder. It can come simply from unexpectedly becoming the centre of attention. You're talking to someone at a social event and gradually realize that everyone else has gone quiet and you've been inadvertently communicating to a group. You don't need to have said anything controversial or ill-judged to feel awkward. Being made visible when you are not ready, involuntary exposure by itself, can create awkwardness and evokes the newly naked Adam and Eve; we want to curl our bodies in on ourselves, with nowhere to turn. Like children covering their faces, we like to be covered up while being able to see, peeking through our fingers. Eye-contact avoiders have a painful tendency to try to cover up in full view, thereby revealing themselves as helplessly exposed in the eye of an audience.

It can also be awkward simply when the wrong person turns up, forcing you to act in ways that don't quite fit the situation. As the sociologist William Cooley puts it:

We are ashamed to seem evasive in the presence of a straightforward man, cowardly in the presence of a brave one, gross in the eyes of a refined one, and so on. We always imagine, and in imagining share, the judgments of the other mind. A man will boast to one person of an action – say some sharp transaction in trade – which he would be ashamed to own to another.[6]

The hyper-social animal that we are is so attuned to 'the judgements of the other mind' that we've developed a range of social emotions to guide us, and some of that guidance, like physical pain, does its work through creating the aversions of social pain. While some emotions – such as sadness, fear, joy, surprise or disgust – can be observed in small babies, the more social ones, such as guilt, embarrassment, shame, envy or pride – appear much later.[7] As we enter the social world, tiptoeing through expectations and judgements, these social emotions help us to navigate our way through situations and relationships without losing face.

Evolutionists interested in how the social emotions came to evolve have suggested that blushing is an important signal, all the more for being involuntary, that you recognize and acknowledge the *faux pas* you have just committed. These emotional cues help you to be seen as a trustworthy person in social groups in which it is very important to know who can be relied upon. The speculation is that social emotions, inconvenient as they may be, developed to signal trustworthiness crucially because they are painful and hard to control. In effect, they are guarantors of our sincerity and suggest we are not merely being manipulative or tactical with cheap talk. And if we don't recognize and repair our awkward moments this way we risk losing face more permanently. Embarrassment, for example, was nicely described by Goffman as being a form of apology or appeasement, such that the embarrassed person 'demonstrates that he/she is at least disturbed by the fact and may prove worthy at another time'.[8] If the proposed face you present, to which you have become so attached, is not held up in the judgement of others, this brings on shame. Our sociometers are like antenna constantly tracking the risk of this in the knowledge that to lose face can be crippling.

I think Erving Goffman would have relished the great TV comedy *Fawlty Towers*. As I read him, I keep picturing the travails of Basil Fawlty with his ever-malfunctioning sociometer. Take the episode called 'Gourmet Night'. Basil decides to upgrade the clientele at Fawlty Towers by arranging the fateful gourmet night to show off his new chef. On the night (which he had advertised in the ever-so-classy *Horse and Hound*, insisting on 'no riff raff') his snobby pretensions are constantly punctured, with Basil constantly failing to project the debonair self-image he feels his illustrious guests demanded. In one scene before the fateful dinner, we can watch him unable to introduce his guests to each other – two grand couples, the Twychens and Colonel and Mrs

Hall. Not knowing the pronunciation of Twychen, thinking it is 'Twitchen', Basil is confronted by a dilemma because Mr Twychen has a very pronounced and distracting twitch, which throws Basil off at the crucial moment. (I've just labelled Basil's comments in this scene, rather than those of the Twychens' and Halls', for ease of reading.)

BASIL May I offer you a little aperitif while you make up your mind what you'd like for dinner?

That's very kind of you.

Lotte? A tomato juice, please.

BASIL Mr Twitchen?

Tomato juice for me, thank you.

BASIL Ah, good! Oh, Colonel. Colonel and Mrs Hall may I introduce [Mr Twychen twitches] Mr. ... And Mrs Tw ...

Have you met?

No, no, we haven't.

BASIL – Have you? – No. Oh, good. What would you like to drink then?

– What?

BASIL – To drink.

I didn't catch the name.

BASIL Oh, you didn't it catch it. What a rotten bit of luck.

– Well?

BASIL – Fine, thank you. And you?

No, no, we still don't know the name.

BASIL Oh, Fawlty, Basil Fawlty.

No, no, theirs!

BASIL   Oh, theirs! So sorry! I thought you meant yours!
My, it's nice and warm, isn't it? I could do with a drink,
too. So, another sherry?
Well, aren't you going to introduce us?

BASIL   – Didn't I? – No! Oh. This is Mr … And Mrs.
What?

BASIL   Uh, Mister and Missus. [*Falls flat on his back.*] Sorry,
I fainted. Well, I feel better now. I'll just get all your tomato
juices.

So as to intensify the feeling of shame, and the comedy of
embarrassment, Basil's interlocutors (apart from the redoubtable
Polly) do nothing to help him out of his conversational
predicaments. In real life we are highly dependent on others
sparing our blushes and consider them heartless if they allow
someone to fail so floridly.

There's another point in a scene where Basil is so panicked
he forgets his own name and his wife Sybil has to remind him.
In Goffman's words, a 'felt lack of judgemental support from the
encounter may take him aback, confuse him and momentarily
incapacitate him as an interactant. His manner and bearing may
falter, collapse and crumble. He may become embarrassed and
chagrined; he may become shamefaced'.

The public lines we take need to go smoothly if social
interaction is to succeed. If not, a comedy of errors, or worse,
ensues. And we call those, like Sacha Baron Cohen's character
Borat, who do not fear such social failure, 'shameless'.

As with many examples of the comedy of embarrassment, Basil's pratfalls are all the more poignant since his humiliations come from believing in his own inferiority. This is a theme that will reappear throughout this book. Social pain links often to a lack of social power, or potency. The process is much more extreme if the line being potentially discredited is being taken by someone with power or prestige. That's why everyone laughs at the boss's lame jokes. And now I wince to picture how ingratiating I become towards mirthless officers, however inane their questions, when going through immigration to get into the United States.

Embarrassment and awkwardness are disproportionately influential given their actual effects. But the effects are passing. Awkward situations, if they don't happen too often, are eventually things we can retell and laugh about in retrospect. Often we retell the experience at our own expense but with a narrative control that the original embarrassing moment never had.

Shame and guilt

Of the various social emotions that police our behaviour, the two that could be singled out as the most powerful responses to social judgement are guilt and shame. They carry far more weight than embarrassment. The awkwardness of walking around with food stains on your shirt may make you blush, but it doesn't invite moral judgement. Where moral judgement is at stake, shame and guilt can follow. And while we might laugh at an embarrassing incident, shame and guilt are no laughing matter.

Shame is different from guilt even though the terms are sometimes used interchangeably to convey accusation, as in 'you should be ashamed of yourself for doing that'. But look more closely and you can see the differences. Shame has more to do with losing face in general; where some stigma, over which you have little control, is exposed to the gaze of others. It leads us to act by hiding, to try to escape the viewer and disappear. We say, 'I wanted the floor to open and swallow me up.'

The writer and researcher Brené Brown describes shame as the fear of disconnection in her *TED Talk* 'Listening to Shame'. She says it makes you ask 'Is there something about me, that if people know it or see it, will make me unworthy of connection?'[9] and believes this is a universal worry. She suggests that people who don't talk about it often end up experiencing it more. By pushing away the acceptance of vulnerability and building highly defended walls of self-protection we can end up all the more fragile, and paradoxically more vulnerable. The thought 'I'm not x enough' plagues almost everyone in some setting or other, where x stands for pretty, tall, clever, educated, serious, witty, original, refined, brave, well-mannered, light-hearted … the list is endless. In order to connect you need to be seen, but shame shadows that need for visibility, because to be seen is to have your stigma made visible, the painfully bright searchlight, spotlight or torchlight which leads to being seen as unqualified, or unsuitable or just ugly. The pain of being seen in this way creates the urge to cover up, or wanting the earth to swallow us up.

By contrast, guilt can't be avoided by hiding or covering up. The internal voice of conscience and self-criticism tells you that you are failing to measure up to the standard you ought to have met. While shame blames the whole person, the sinner, guilt focuses merely on their sin and therefore enables more options for fixing the problem. It implies autonomy and agency in that if you chose to transgress in a certain way and were fairly judged for doing so, this means you can choose again to do something about it. Shame, on the other hand, feels more like a wholesale judgement about something you have less control over and therefore cannot repair.

We are sometimes ashamed of things that are not our fault and humiliated despite our good intentions. These differ from pure guilt, where we are caught out for knowingly being in the wrong. These stigmata police our sense of self. Think of how embarrassed people can feel by some aspect of their physical appearance that cannot be concealed. 'They are emotions connected with the worth of selves, or character. But when we dwell on that which humiliates us we do not become angry with ourselves; rather, we are repelled by our own "ugliness."'[10]

For psychologists June Price Tangney and Ronda L. Dearing in their book *Shame and Guilt*, shame experiences the whole self as under attack and it not only triggers a challenge to self-worth and the need to hide, but more disturbingly this can lead to a lack of empathy and a proneness to anger. Guilt suggests 'I did a bad thing' while shame concludes 'I am a bad person', so the former drives you to criticize yourself and to atone. It creates the need for reparation to alleviate the harm caused, by focusing on the victim.

Guilt is in a sense much more adaptive and morally useful since it triggers the need to repair, and requires empathy to know how to do that. One way to think of this is by considering what might be the opposite of these negative social emotions. For Tangney and Dearing, the opposite of guilt is pride, while the opposite of shame is hubris. For these kinds of reasons, in moral philosophy guilt is often thought of as a more mature and progressive form of moral thinking. It is less dependent on generalized norms, and results more from an awareness of harm caused to others. If guilt focuses you more on the victim of your wrongdoing, you are thereby more oriented towards doing something about it. Shame, on the other hand, invites looking in on the failure of yourself, and to being less aware of others as a consequence.

Imagine a soldier returning from a war in which he had committed appalling acts. The possibility for reconciliation is greater if he feels guilt rather than shame about his conduct. If he purely felt shame he might hide away hoping to bury the memories and never speak of them. By contrast, someone feeling guilty might seek to make amends, be open to truth and reconciliation; and perhaps we might wish to help an individual, or indeed a nation, move through a predominance of shame towards guilt (even collective guilt) so that this in turn might move towards atonement, even forgiveness. In the last twenty years we have seen the relatively new phenomenon of the national apology in which the collective guilt from crimes of the past are acknowledged and apologized for by contemporary leaders seeking to make amends.

For this reason many would echo Freud in feeling we couldn't have civilization without guilt. The struggle between ego and super ego enables the self-restraint and reciprocity that are crucial to a functioning society. But guilt can also have destructive effects, if taken too far. It can overreach and lead to harmful consequences. Because there is no blueprint to gauge the right amount of guilt to experience, we can overdo it. When this happens, the tendency is to go beyond self-criticism, which can lead to self-punishment, giving rise to a form of masochism. The self-criticizing voice in your head then becomes deafening. Rather than enabling you to put things right, it becomes paralyzing and slides into shame. Adam Phillips describes the punishing super ego as a person who, if you met them, would lead you to think 'what a horribly cruel, boring, repetitive judgemental bully. This person must have had some real trouble in life to end up that way'. And, as Phillips adds, 'you'd be right'.[11]

Guilt and shame, while conceptually distinct, are often experienced together. Imagine being caught helping yourself to an extra, and let's say the last, slice of cake, when you thought no one was looking. The feeling you have could combine shades of guilt and shame. The judgement of others might make you feel guilty for being unfair and depriving them of their share, and but also might make you feel ashamed for showing your lack of self-control – the glutton's remorse. The judgements that lead to our feeling guilty for something we had more control over, and shame for something we could not control so well, have similar weight in the end. The harshest judgements combine the two. The gentleman with red whiskers who always went first through a doorway is exposed to ill judgement over his actions and appearance whether he has much control over them or not.[12]

There is research suggesting that more recent Western societies are guilt cultures whereas older, or more collectivist societies, are better described as shame cultures. The origin of this thinking comes from Ruth Benedict, whose 1946 book *The Chrysanthemum and the Sword* contrasted Americans as having a Christian guilt culture with Japanese who were typified as having a shame culture. This is not more than superficially persuasive and probably says more about the acceptable language in environments which emphasize the individual over the collective. Certainly, there is a strong emphasis on 'face' and shame by association in collectivist societies (even to the point of driving people to committing 'honour killings'), but there are no cultures or people who are not prone to shame, even if this less explicitly described. In fact, in some ways a Western liberal tradition with an emphasis on the benefits of transparency may have increased the conditions under which people feel ashamed of themselves. A freedom of information act is a great tool for inconvenient unveilings. And in the digital age we've come to realise we have never been so public, which opens people up to being exposed in so many more ways, as painfully described in Jon Ronson's book *So You've Been Publicly Shamed*. This digital turn can be seen in terms of a shift from a guilt culture where people were once focused on right versus wrong, to a shame culture where the key distinction is whether you have been included and accepted or excluded and rejected from whichever social media grouping is most important to you.

Social emotions, whether around embarrassment resulting from awkwardness through to guilt and shame, do useful work in policing our social behaviour. They provide triggers and aversions, like physical pain or disgust, and therefore help us avoid the pain of isolation and help to maintain the impression that we are trustworthy. In order to successfully avoid those punishments requires more than good intentions. We also need skill.

I was driving from Boston to Maine in New Hampshire many years ago, happily looking forward to staying with a journal editor at his farm, when a police car sounded the siren. He pulled me over and barked at me for a while about speeding. I'd been used to British motorways, I said, with a speed limit of 70 mph, where this US freeway I now realized had a limit of 55 mph. He wasn't interested in this explanation and asked to see my licence. I had one of those old green paper licences that fold up in a plastic wallet. I also forgot that many years before someone had advised me to keep £10 in that folded-up wallet 'for a rainy day' and forget about it. One day I'd need petrol and have no cash and I'd be grateful for this foresight. Well, as the traffic cop started to unfold my licence I realized too late what was going to happen, and hoped somehow it wouldn't show. Within seconds the £10 emerged from the folds with vulgar insistence, and he looked at me, eyes narrowed, and said quietly, 'Are you trying to bribe me, son?'. Somehow in my gibbering spray of denial he recognized a grain of credibility especially when I pointed out that if I was actually trying to bribe him I would have used dollars.

But I think there was another reason he believed me. I came across as ashamed or at least embarrassed rather than guilty. The cack-handed overture, the sheer overtness, just isn't how things like this are done. The main reason this encounter was so excruciating is that the money stuck out so bluntly. If you want to bribe someone, or indeed navigate any conversationally awkward terrain, you had better be more subtle than that, and to learn how to cover it up appropriately. My crass gesture, if it had been intended, would have been plain rude.

Had I been guilty of trying to bribe the officer I don't know whether he would have arrested me or let me off after a suitable confession and apology. Either way I would have been in a position to apologize or pay a fine and make amends for my wrongdoing.

To keep your sociometer scoring high and social pain at bay you need skill. Whenever we say something that suggests your motives (or mine) are dodgy or that your capacity (or mine) is limited, we use indirect speech to avoid awkwardness. A bribe classically impugns your motives or mine and so I don't say 'If I give you money, will you let me off the speeding ticket?', I say 'Surely we can sort this out another way.' Your aggressive kid is high-spirited, and your meanness with money best left unsaid. Without veiled speech too many people might sound like Sacha Baron Cohen's Borat, who once asked a fellow dinner guest, 'When can I have sex with you?'. We rarely speak directly in touchy or dodgy situations and so instead we cover up.

Covering up

I go to the gym each week with two t-shirts. After forty-five minutes sweating away on a cross-trainer, it's time to change before carrying on with weights. My local gym is part of a complex, which means you walk beside the large indoor pool to get to the changing rooms. I used to go to the changing rooms, but have latterly taken to changing shirts beside the pool instead of heading over to the lockers and back. What strikes me every time is that this is a borderline experience. It doesn't feel quite right. Changing in the changing rooms would be uncontroversial, clearly, and stripping off my shirt in the gym itself would equally clearly be out of order. But there is an ambiguous space by the pool. On one level the fact that none of the men in or by the pool is wearing a top means there's no problem for me to take off my shirt. On another, I'm clearly someone in gym kit, rather than a swimmer, and the very act of changing beside the pool is an unveiling, which somehow makes me want to do it quickly and unobtrusively. Obviously, it doesn't bother me enough to go all the way to the changing room, but it does hurry me along. And even if it is on the right side of acceptable to change shirts by the pool, it wouldn't be if I were a woman, would it?

We are continually making choices about clothing and unclothing ourselves, both literally and metaphorically. Most of the time we can ignore this fact, like the fish that does not notice the water in which it is suspended. But this does not mean we can act as though no one is watching, even if that is a somewhat disturbing thought at times. Borderline cases such as my t-shirt changing moment are the ones that help to reveal the invisible pressures that shape our way in the world, and the impressions we need to manage.

The most acute observer in this regard is the sociologist Erving Goffman for whom 'the world, in truth, is a wedding'. Goffman distinguished between front staging areas and back stage to describe the dramaturgical self with unnerving acuity. He identified the subtle cues and micro-management we indulge in so as to come off as a less stigmatized self. For instance, why does it seem that, in a public place, a person will check her watch more often than necessary while waiting for a tardy friend. It is not just that she is checking the time; there is also the trace of communication to others that she is waiting. The invisible codes need to be understood if we are to be culturally literate and to avoid making a gaffe. We dress in private and do so with knowledge of what is needed to be suitable before facing the world.

It is easy to imagine that this means we wear masks in public to cover our true selves hiding beneath. But Goffman was careful to point out that our backstage selves, the ones where we behave without an audience, are no more authentic than the publicly orientated front. The tendency to separate these two into 'mask' and 'face' is based on an inaccurate idea that some true version can be uncovered. By contrast, for Goffman our masks run deep. Often they represent the person we would genuinely like to be and shape our behaviour as we strive to live up to that reputation.

Clothed or unclothed, we constantly choose what to reveal or conceal in social settings. And what is true of our physical selves is just as relevant in our forms of speech. While we sometimes think of language as a transparent window of communication, in truth we are boxing much cleverer than that and usually by communicating indirectly, artfully and between the lines. Veiling our language is as significant in social settings as veiling our bodies.

A compelling exploration of why and how we use indirect speech comes from the psychologist Steven Pinker.[13] He starts with a puzzle about uncontroversial exchanges. Why do we tiptoe and finagle our way through perfectly obvious situations, when a direct approach would seem to save everyone time? How odd that someone would utter 'If you could pass the guacamole, that would be awesome' rather than just 'Pass me the guacamole.' Politeness certainly requires that even a direct request is softened with a 'please' and acknowledged with a 'thanks'. But politeness can't really explain examples like these. Pinker offers that there is something deeper going on which turns on the fact that human relationships are an admixture of cooperativeness and conflict to varying degrees, and indirect speech is needed to navigate this fact.

To develop his idea, he focuses on touchy situations where indirect speech is rife such as sexual come-ons (I only need mention the word 'etchings'), threats ('Nice place you got here, shame if something should happen to it') and, of course, bribery ('Sorry I was speeding officer, perhaps we can just sort this out here somehow').

His theory has three interlocking parts, each of which is revealing. The first draws on game theory to explain why *plausible deniability* can be so valuable under certain conditions. The second itemizes the *kinds of relationships* we can have with others (a boss becomes a friend, a friend becomes a business partner, etc.) and what we need to do to slide between these expectations without awkwardness. The final part is around the importance of avoiding *common knowledge* in touchy situations. Put the three together and we get some genuine insight into how and why we need the skill of indirect speech and equal insight into why comedies like *Fawlty Towers* or *The Office* are so excruciating to watch.

There are three drivers of indirect speech.

1. Plausible deniability: The economist Thomas Schelling was the first to recognize the important of diplomacy in a case where you cannot be sure of the values of your interlocutor. That's to say if you are not sure of what the other person will think of your needs, wants or motives, you need to tread carefully. Pinker applies this insight to map out the options that would be available to someone like me and that traffic cop in Boston. So let's imagine I did in fact want to bribe him. If I were to use direct speech, 'If I give you money will you let me off?', I force one of two options. If the cop is dishonest, then the bribe works and I'm let off; if he's honest, the bribe fails and I get arrested.

But if I use indirect speech, then more options open up thanks to plausible deniability. That is, the honest cop may know what I'm getting at but doesn't quite have the certainty to make it stand up in court due to the test of reasonable doubt. So, in a case where I don't know whether the cop is honest or not (if they're all dishonest I should be blunt and do the deal, if all honest then don't even try it), it pays to be diplomatic and hope for the best. Worst case you just get rebuffed and pay the fine.

This logic drives the need for plausible deniability under the right conditions of uncertainty and differing vantage points.

2. Kinds of relationships: Indirect speech also arises from managing across differing types of relationships. When you think of it, the ridiculous guacamole request is an attempt not to sound bossy to a friend, two quite distinct ways of relating to each other. Pinker draws here on the work of the anthropologist Alan Fiske to detail the key relationship types that occur repeatedly in our lives and which bring with them certain expectations of common interest and expectations.

The first type of relationship Fiske calls 'mutuality'. This is the 'what's mine is thine', kith and kin type of bond. It's why you can just help yourself to the food on your partner's plate (sometimes!) in the way you would not with a stranger. Persuaders of various stripes will try to evoke this mutual bond by physical touching, or using the language of family, 'Hey, brother, can you spare some change', as a way to prompt us to share.

The second relationship type is reciprocal. In this case, the logic is more around fair exchange than mutuality. In essence, you scratch my back and I'll scratch yours. When you divide the pie into equal portions or respond with tit-for-tat exchanges you are operating with this relationship type in mind. Charities and salespeople will often give something away for 'free' so as to trigger the sense that we ought, in fairness, to give something in return.

The third relationship type in this model is known as 'authority ranking', which allows the imposition of blunt will, for example, 'do what I say', etc.[14] It is often a test of strength and seniority and what's going on when you say 'don't mess with me'. Think of any organization with a hierarchy where this kind of relationship is at its most unambiguous. In this case, there is a clear power differential between people and requisite (sometimes contractual) expectations of the roles they occupy.

We all have relationships of these kinds with others and have an intuitive sense of which is in play at any one time. The value of indirect speech is in how it helps out when you have to navigate the borders of these relationships. We can see the difficulty in the slide from mutuality to reciprocal relationships, for example when close friends enter into a business transaction together which doesn't work out well. People at work who are friendly with each other need sometimes to reflect the power relations they may have toward each other and this requires diplomatic skill on both sides, shifting as it does between these relationship types. I'll explore diplomatic speech in a work context in more detail shortly.

3. Common knowledge: Another driver of indirect speech is the need to avoid common knowledge. This is a technical concept in logic and differs from mere shared knowledge. Shared knowledge comes about where I know something and you know something but I can't be sure that you know that I know. The extra step that we can take where I now know that you know that I know and so on is a recursive explosion of common knowledge. Pinker's favourite example is the story of the emperor's new clothes. As the emperor walks into the crowded hall with no clothes, everyone individually can see that he is wearing nothing. That is, I can see and you can see, but I can't be sure that you can see what I can see. At this point we have mere shared knowledge. That is until the little boy shouts out 'He's naked!'. The power of that public signal sets off the chain reaction of common knowledge. Now not only do I know he's naked and you know he's naked but I know that you know he's naked, and you know that I know that you know, etc., etc.

This is why dictators so often divide and conquer. There is great collective and possibly revolutionary power in common knowledge. How does this relate to our need for indirect speech in touchy situations? Well, it is the demand for plausible deniability again. In our versions of indirectness we can keep a discreet veil over what happened and remain friends even if the hint was rebuffed; even if the veil is pretty transparent. If the veil is removed then there is no escape from mutual knowledge. Pinker draws on a scene from the film *When Harry Met Sally* to illustrate such an unveiling.

After their long car journey together, Harry and Sally are having dinner (with Sally memorably ordering in her fussy high maintenance mode). Suddenly Harry begins:

HARRY   You're a very attractive person.

SALLY   Thank you.

HARRY   Amanda never said how attractive you were.

SALLY   Well maybe she doesn't think I'm attractive.

HARRY   I don't think it's a matter of opinion, empirically you are attractive.

SALLY   Amanda is my friend.

HARRY   So?

SALLY   So you're going with her.

HARRY   So?

SALLY   So you're coming on to me!

HARRY   No I wasn't. What?

HARRY   Can't a man say a woman is attractive without it being a come-on?
Alright, alright, let's just say just for the sake of argument that it was a come-on. What do you want me to do about it? I take it back, ok? I take it back.

SALLY   You can't take it back.

HARRY   Why not?

SALLY   Because it's already out there.

HARRY   Oh Jeez, what are we supposed to do, call the cops?
It's already out there.

Once it is out there we can't take things back, and so veiled speech can contain the awkwardness that leads to embarrassment, shame or ridicule. Of course, when we deploy technique the process is more supple and subtle and less conscious than all this implies.

I often think of this need for clever footwork in an office setting. I recently had to fill out some 360-degree questionnaires about the 'management effectiveness' of various of my colleagues. And I was struck by how emphatically the document offers anonymity. 'Your responses will be kept **completely confidential**; your name will not be associated with your responses.' As the reassurance implies, uncovered, unvarnished speech at work is risky business.

Why would this be? To get by in life we need to square circles. We need to manage conflicting priorities, needs and wants – both in ourselves and in others. Some of those motives are flattering and some are not. The parts of us that are lazy, selfish, weak-willed or short-term compete with our better angels. We are torn by contradictory desires, whether around status, money, sex, escapism or love and affection; we want to be fair-minded *and* fulfilled, to fit in *and* to stand out, we want to party with friends *and* spend time with the kids, an easy life *and* to 'do our bit'. Our contradictory desires need to be ironed out into a coherent seeming self despite the fact that contradictory desires make this impossible.

The awkward fact is that your needs and mine don't converge as much as we pretend. And so, in pursuit of credibility, we contrive to get our stories sounding straighter than we are. Think of all this in a work setting, where the stakes are so high and the motives so mixed. A commonplace reminder of the silent calculations we have to make comes up in the sick feeling you get when you've hit *send* on a tricky email too quickly. Did you copy in the client who you were moaning about to your best friend? Work dials up the tension because relationships are governed by power and money, and so reputations have real consequences. Losing credibility at work can mean losing your job. So an office is filled with cover-ups.

And when power and money loom larger, the stakes get higher and the concealments become all the more tempting or necessary. CEOs of public companies have particular tensions to manage. Propaganda declaimed in lofty tones – 'people are our number one resource' – habitually conceals the fact that the primary task is to make faceless shareholders (usually financial investors who can pull the plug in a moment) a profit, and often generates the cynicism it deserves. Yet these contradictions are inevitable to some degree – as someone once said: no margin, no mission. Even NGOs need to work out how to pursue their goals while keeping the lights on and their employees paid. I've often felt sorry for estate agents, politicians and double-glazing salespeople who suffer that knowing chuckle, simply because they negotiate conflicting interests out in the open. Their need to persuade is painfully clear to see. Others (doctors, publishers, academics) can be more discreet, but beware complacent assumptions. No one with a product or a service to offer, or a reputation to manage, can get by without spin of one kind or another.

Of course, we do speak transparently most of the time. When someone asks you where the toilets are, or what time it is, you don't tend to call up the silky skills of impression management. You just answer the question. It's just that when the stakes are high the simple truth isn't a simple option. We have choices to make. When your boss asks you how you're feeling you might not choose to mention the horrendous hangover that has left you unable to see straight, or maybe you will. But either way you're unlikely to answer as unselfconsciously as you would to the friend who kept you up drinking the night before. Context is all. This is why the 360-degree survey stresses that my anonymity is guaranteed. The reassurance is there to say 'don't worry about the consequences of telling the truth *this* time, just tell it like you see it'.

But even this cloak of anonymity doesn't guarantee transparency. Am I being as unvarnished as I think I am when filling out the form? Isn't there a danger I might exaggerate scores or diminish them for unconscious but self-serving reasons? I don't think I am, but that doesn't mean I'm not. This is because we are blessed with mechanisms of self-deception that keep uncomfortable truths at bay. Lying consciously is difficult for most people and detected fairly easily, so the most successful liars have already convinced themselves. In our need for a flattering self-image we underestimate the quiet covering up that abounds in adult life – the deluded brain can't see itself fooling itself. Research reveals that doctors think 84 per cent of their colleagues will be influenced by freebies from pharmaceutical companies, while only 16 per cent say they would be similarly influenced.[15] Apparently only the depressed are realistic in their self-image, rather than busy overestimating and spinning like everyone else.[16] This 'depressive realism' is shown in studies where people are asked to rank themselves on various criteria and then compare those scores with the way others would judge them on the same criteria. It turns out the most of us have a rose-tinted 'optimism bias', which helps us to imagine we are better than average at many things, from driving to parenting.

In any case, cover stories aren't always a bad thing. Yes, we have interests to serve and reputations to protect, but these motives aren't always malign; they cover a spectrum from selfish to noble. Of course, there are exploitative deceptions, like falsely accusing someone, or taking the credit for a colleague's work. But there are milder forms of dissimulation too: pretending that a job took you ages when it didn't, or that it was a breeze when you burned the midnight oil, or guffawing heartily at the boss's lame wit. These lack integrity admittedly, but are not so harmful (unless you've been charging the client for those imaginary extra hours). And there are plenty of ordinary or convenient deceptions that do no particular harm such as good manners and politeness. We feign interest in a colleague's hobbies – 'So when exactly does the ultimate frisbee season start?' – or pleasure on opening an unsuitable present – 'Gosh, that's so kind of you! You really shouldn't have.' There are kind-spirited 'white' lies motivated by loyalty or modesty, and even heroic lies such as taking the fall for someone else who you know will be unfairly punished.

Equally, speaking too plainly or too bluntly can be stupid or have unintended consequences. Gerald Ratner, the owner of a downmarket jewellery business, committed a diplomatic malfunction by describing his £4.99 decanter as 'total crap' and compounding the problem by describing a pair of earrings as 'cheaper than an M&S prawn sandwich but probably wouldn't last as long', which nearly destroyed his company. And who applauds the colleague for calling people ugly or stupid just because he happens to believe it is true? As Tennessee Williams once commented, 'all cruel people pride themselves on being paragons of frankness'. The judgement of whether I find you trustworthy is not a simple assessment of whether you tell the truth all the time. It is more about whether you are well-motivated in what you choose to say. Rather than being faithful to the bare facts, I'm counting on you to factor in at least a need to be faithful to me, my hopes or aspirations or self-image.

And, as we've seen, you need the skill to communicate this in the right way, which often means indirectly. When doing someone's appraisal you can speak pretty clearly about 'strengths' but weaknesses are better described, for those who find the word makes them feel queasy, as 'development needs'. You can spray good news around in an unfocused way and it will be lapped up uncritically. 'You're such a great person', 'That was amazing' and similarly sugary sentiments are consumed uncritically, while criticism had better be pretty specific (separating the sin from the sinner) if it is going to be heard, let alone accepted. This is partly because criticism has much more impact than praise and is likely to generate defensive rebuttals.

The level of skill we can bring to the need for indirect implication varies enormously from careless speakers like Gerald Ratner at one end through to the skilled daily labours of journalists and politicians at the other. An opinion piece written by *Guardian* columnist Jonathan Freedland that assessed George Osborne's 2015 budget, much heralded for being 'politically astute', illustrates some of this fancy footwork at different levels. Freedland watches Osborne attempting to pull off a trick. By announcing a national minimum wage (while pulling benefits from the working poor), he was continuing a project of 'compassionate conservativism' that started with David Cameron's own efforts to detoxify the brand of the 'nasty party'. As Freedland observes,

> it was not the poor he was wooing. He wanted the votes of those who care about the poor, or more accurately those who don't like to think they're the sort of person who doesn't care.

In this subtle assessment we see here that Freedland is judging Osborne's judgement of voters' preferences. And Freedland's judgement splits into two. On the one hand, Osborne is demonstrating political skill, while on the other hand betraying cynical motives. His judgement, in Freedland's view, on who should be helped was not based not so much on need as political value.

Freedland decides, 'The cynical person here is Osborne himself. He is making a judgment about the limits of sympathy the majority of the electorate have for those falling behind.' He also concludes that Osborne's calculation is basically correct. And that 'Labour should be watching and learning.'

This is a skilful assessment that hides its own controversial assumptions in a persuasive tone of reasonableness. Freedland offers the supposedly obvious truth that 'voting is not an act of charity, but of self-interest' with a world-weary shrug, and points out that the opposition Labour politicians need to get this point if they are to compete with the Tories. But this claim is not uncontroversial and could be countered. Political scientists make a distinction between voters voting for instrumental reasons versus for expressive ones.[17] The former are in line with Freedland's assumption that people vote out of self-interest, while the latter reasons are about signalling who the voters are and what they value. The rise of Labour under Jeremy Corbyn on a platform of compassion rather than self-interest shows that Freedland's assumption is not inevitable. Freedland is careful though. He, for instance, qualifies his claims (and thus himself) with rebuttals of possible objections and with knowledge of what a *Guardian* readership will expect from their fellow travelling columnist. So even as he argues that voters are motivated by self-interest, he qualifies this claim by saying 'even if that self-interest includes the kind of society you want to live in'. This then redefines the concept of self-interest so widely as to be unobjectionable and extendable to include all voting populations of whichever political hue (from Glasgow to Texas, from Athens to Berlin).

See how skilfully Freedland judges Osborne and how he does so in a way that deflects possible judgement of him. This is, of course, what any professional commentator should be able to do. But it is fairly clear that the withering insights the judge offers on the judged are rarely directed at themselves to the same degree. And this of course is true of how I'm judging Freedland.

The evaluation of others' motives and skills comes to us almost effortlessly and frequently outside of our conscious attention. What we do less well is apply this test to ourselves. The biblical imprecation to note the beam in your own eye before messing with the speck in someone else's is a valuable reminder that we don't always apply the same standards of scrutiny to ourselves. So, when I read the Freedland article I don't think too hard about the quiet satisfactions I get from seeing what he is up to, while feeling quite uninhibited in assessing his assessment of Osborne. And I don't think too clearly about whether the actual point he is making about voters needing consciences salved before pursuing their self-interest applies to me. Who are these voters Osborne has manipulated so cynically with his fig leaves anyway? Easy for me to imagine others to whom this applies, but am I willing to imagine it might apply to me?

The business of managing impressions is a subtle and complex one, and is much of the time unconscious, especially for those who are lucky enough to be well versed in the codes or norms of a given culture. But this familiarity and therefore the options available for managing impressions are not evenly distributed.

Making an impression

My father was born and grew up in Jordan and went to school at Baghdad College in Iraq. When it came to approaching higher education, he was advised by his father to go to England to do 'A' levels and get a degree. Following that advice, he boarded a plane from Amman to London in the summer of 1957. His first impressions are telling. When he landed at Heathrow and looked out at the runway and the buildings sluiced with water, he was impressed by how thoroughly everything had been washed down. After all, if the streets of Amman are soaked it is because people have been sloshing bucket-loads of water down them to get rid of dust. It simply didn't occur to him that it had been raining in late August.

When he arrived at Waterloo on a bus from the airport with two suitcases, he asked directions to Piccadilly to find his lodgings, and was told to go 'north of the river'. So, he grabbed his cases and set off on foot assuming he just had a river to cross. Sweating after walking for a good while, and still not arriving, it dawned on him that he really was on unfamiliar ground. The next morning, he needed to go to Norwood to register at his college and asked how to get there. He was advised to get the train, which baffled him because his father had insisted the college was in London. You would only get a train in Amman to go to another town.

His experience must speak for many who have had to find their way in new terrain. There is a scene in Sam Selvon's short novel *The Lonely Londoners* describing the immigration of Caribbean men to London in the 1950s:

'Come and catch a bus,' Moses say, and he take Galahad to the bus queue. When the bus come, Galahad pushing in front of the other people though Moses try to hold him back, and the conductor say, 'Ere, you can't break the queue like that, mate.' And Galahad had to stand up and watch all the people who was there before him get on the bus, and a old lady look at him with a loud tone in her eye, and a girl tell a fellar she was with: 'They'll have to learn to do better, you know.'[18]

My father was equally baffled by queuing and no doubt triggered that silently 'loud tone' in many eyes. He remarks on how the English would line up in orderly fashion hoping to get a ticket to the cinema. And if the line was too long, the one who missed out would just go home disappointed. In Amman, by contrast, Friday night at the movies was a more chaotic thing, where, as he told it, 'I would usually lose a couple of buttons off my shirt' in the scramble for tickets.

While queuing is in robust health still, we don't seem to queue for buses any longer. There are small courtesies about who you let on the bus to avoid that unspoken 'loud tone' of disapproval but it's not based on who got to the bus stop first anymore. Cultural norms get updated after all. It takes an anthropological eye to turn these familiar unspoken assumptions into a visible and interpretable view. Kate Fox has done just this in her book *Watching the English*. She is sharp-eyed enough to show that even in the apparently haphazard non-queuing attempt to buy a drink in a pub by bellying up to the bar, there is a world of invisible code in play which she dubs 'the pantomime rule'. In this 'invisible queue' she sees a strict etiquette required to negotiate the mutual recognition (unvoiced eye-contact with the person behind bar) that gets you a drink.

> It is acceptable to let bar staff know one is waiting to be served by holding money or an empty glass in one's hand. The pantomime rule allows us to tilt the empty glass, or perhaps turn it slowly in a circular motion … The etiquette here is frighteningly precise: it is permitted to perch one's elbow on the bar, for example, with either money or an empty glass in a raised hand but not to raise a whole arm and wave the notes or glass around [and requires] the adoption of an expectant, hopeful, even slightly anxious expression

You can't look too complacent:

> those waiting to be served must stay alert and keep their eye on the bar staff at all times. Once eye contact is made, a quick lift of the eyebrows, sometimes accompanied by an upward jerk of the chin, and a hopeful smile, lets the staff know you are waiting.
>
> The English perform this pantomime instinctively, without being aware of following a rigid etiquette, and never question the extraordinary handicaps (no speaking, no waving, no noise, constant alertness to subtle non-verbal signals) imposed by the rule.[19]

Perhaps this explains my own lack of bar presence.

The uninitiated must be daunted by the complexity. Fox comments that an Italian family sitting at their table for a good while eventually got up and left the pub, assuming no one was going to serve them.

In looking closely at the pantomime rule, Kate Fox has given us an example of what anthropologists call 'thick description'. The term was coined by the philosopher Gilbert Ryle, who described the difference between a twitch (a mere physical flicker of an eyelid) and a wink, saturated in meaning and significance. A thin description settles for a mere physical description of what happened, while a thick description recognizes that a wink does a lot more than that and is an attempt to read into the silent messages (mockery, innuendo, comedy?) contained therein.

We need to be careful readers of our culture to become capable of the meaning-saturated thick descriptions that social life provides every day. Most of this skill comes from thousands of interactions over time which deepens a sense of place and belonging. We need to read people and the cultures they inhabit effectively if we are to find our footing and save face in the knowledge that we are always prone to the possibility of the false note, the gaffe and the corresponding judgement that comes from not following, or at least knowing, the rules.[20] So any judgement we might receive is highly contextualized by the innumerable secret codes and unwritten rules that enmesh our social reality. Like a cat burglar negotiating a laser beam–filled room to avoid setting off the alarm, we have to become skilled at avoiding getting things wrong.

And quite often the alarm is set off silently, or in a way so encoded as to make it clear to all watching but not necessarily to the victim of this hard assessment. We don't always note the 'loud tone' in people's eyes. Listen to Richard Feynman, the physicist, gradually learning the sound of harsh judgement after he moved from the engineering-friendly MIT to graduate school at Princeton where more airs and graces were expected.

> I go through the door, and there are some ladies, and some girls, too. It's all very formal and I'm thinking where to sit down and should I sit next to this girl, or not, and how should I behave, when I hear a voice behind me.
>
> 'Would you like cream or lemon in your tea, Mr Feynman?' It's Miss Eisenhart pouring tea.
>
> 'I'll have both, thank you,' I say, still looking for where I'm going to sit, when suddenly I hear 'heh-heh-heh-heh-heh. Surely you're joking, Mr Feynman.'
>
> Joking? Joking? What the hell did I just say? Then I realised what I had done. That was my first experience with this tea business.
>
> Later on, after I had been at Princeton longer, I got to understand this heh-heh-heh-heh-heh. In fact it was at that first tea, as I was leaving, that I realised what it meant. 'You're making a social error.' Because the next time I heard this same cackle, 'heh-heh-heh-heh-heh', from Miss Eisenhart, someone was kissing her hand as he left.[21]

Today Feynman would presumably be doing a lot better. Western culture has become less formal and more accommodating of different norms. And of course, the tech-savvy, the self-professed 'geeks', in the wake of the giant success of big technology companies, have taken over the world. So, a physicist would be more lauded now than in the age of C. P. Snow's 'two cultures' when the scientist was relegated to second-class citizen in favour of more literary types.[22] Now that engineering is the more dominant intellectual metaphor of our age, you're more likely to commit a social error and hear that 'cackle' for being too fancy, formal or fusty. While Feynman might approve, this would not be an example of a world free of judgement; there is still as complex a web of meaning and judgement to negotiate. The title of his sequel to *Surely You're Joking, Mr Feynman* was *What Do You Care What Other People Think?*. This came out of an exchange with his wife Arlene and was a reminder to her not to be too swayed by the views of others. But rather than deleting her judging audience he was merely substituting it for another audience, namely himself. She needed to care about how he thought of her caring what other people think. There is no escape. There is no version of culture which isn't strewn with codes and rules and that can keep us off balance and anxious about fitting in.

Why does Basil Fawlty make our toes curl? Why do we call the show 'painfully' funny? Through Basil's incompetence, we can see how life would look if we were less skilled at managing impressions. The embarrassment we feel is not about double standards and self-delusion – we all have those. It's that those contradictions are poking out for all to see. Without the dramatic skill to keep up a polished, convincing front, Basil is committing the crime of *revealing* his more crudely motivated backstage machinery. Walking around with your flies down isn't awkward because of what you *reveal* – it's that you've failed to *conceal*. And so it is with all of us – we're expected to conceal our dirty laundry and mixed motives (hopefully so well we can all believe there's nothing to hide).

Why are some people considered 'cool' and others 'gauche', why are some 'charismatic' and others 'clumsy'? Pick your term. There is a never-ending stream of small appraisals of these kinds being made. Importantly, people considered 'cool' look like they can succeed without trying and seem to fail without caring. Apparently indifferent to danger and to consequences, cool people crucially, as Feynman demanded, don't seem to care what other people think. This is understandably appealing and a great illusion to conjure up, since we judge people for being too obvious in their desire to court good judgement.[23]

Interestingly, there is a difference between how people with low self-esteem manage impressions as contrasted with people with high self-esteem. They both look for flattering light but the latter are looking to shine brighter, while the former are preoccupied with avoiding coming across badly. The psychologist Roy Baumeister offers that low self-esteem is a state of mind that 'is based on protecting oneself from failure, embarrassment, rejection and humiliation, whereas high self-esteem entails an ... orientation based on enhancing one's prestige and reputation for competence'.[24] If we worry more about hiding our clay feet rather than regarding our fine plumage we have more chance of feeling better about ourselves in the longer run.[25] Contrary to some of the back-slapping advice that we encounter in self-help and business books, if we acknowledge the common lot we share with other impression managers we might benefit from stopping our self-esteem from flying too high.

The coolest of the cool, who never looks like she is trying, should not mislead us; as with any gliding swan, the feet are paddling hard, if invisibly. Even though every swan was once (and occasionally still is) an ugly duckling, self-deception and a healthy sociometer can help conceal this obvious fact. Oscar Wilde may have quipped that the truth is rarely pure and never simple, but we prefer our loftier propaganda, each of us a mini-CEO advertising how well-intentioned and able we really are, and averting our gaze from the machinery humming in the background.[26]

I'm fond of W. H. Auden's line that 'sincerity is technique', an observation that is as unsettling as it is insightful. But to think that credibility depends on skill more than we like to admit makes us a bit queasy. A focus on keeping up appearances can feel like we are degrading our integrity, and caring too much about what other people think, and sometimes on the shallowest of criteria.[27]

The queasiness that comes from needing to make a good impression invites the question of whether it is even possible to be authentic, not least because our self-judgement can be so wildly inaccurate. Where our sincerity requires technique to be appreciated by others, we can easily start to feel inauthentic despite good intentions. We don't want to be defined by what

Adam Smith called the 'quackish arts of self-promotion'. Nor do we want to drift, like Sartre's waiter who is too 'waiteresque' in his ostentatious effort to serve – 'his movement is quick and forward, a little too precise, a little too rapid' – into a state of bad faith. Bad faith was the concept used by Sartre and Simone de Beauvoir to describe an inauthentic denial of the freedom we have to choose while submitting to social forces. The waiter is disowning his freedom by choosing to focus on playing the role. De Beauvoir identifies various forms of bad faith, with the consequent denial of freedom that comes with it, such as the Narcissist who replaces it with construing herself as an object of desire, the Mystic who submits to some absolute, the Woman in Love who submerges her identity into her male partner and the Serious Man who plunges himself into an outside cause. For both Sartre and de Beauvoir believed we are condemned to be free. And however much we occlude this from view with false values that come from adopting such roles we cannot, for them, overturn our fundamental capacity to choose.

Whether or not the existential philosophers are in the end too uncompromising in their demand that we always have the option to act freely, they give us pause with their diagnoses of how we can submerge ourselves into a role and the hollowness that follows from living inauthentically. And this fits with the queasiness I've described. There are however, it seems to me, a couple of correctives to the feeling of hollowness that can come from contemplating how susceptible we are to the judgement of others. The first comes from the fact that there is a limit on how much conscious impression management we can actually pull off. That is to say we may not be in a constant deceptive state because we know how hard it is to fool people. The economist Robert Frank, in a lovely book exploring the strategic role of emotions, *Passions within Reason*, concludes that the safest way to seem good, is in fact to be good. He points out that not only have we evolved to manage impressions, we have also evolved to spot manipulators and so it is difficult to keep up a constant act convincingly. People will find you out. Our emotions evolved, in this light, as guarantors of sincerity precisely because they are hard to fake. So his view is that we should develop characteristics and qualities that are accompanied by the right emotion if we ever truly want to convince others. He reflects on why he pays tips as he leaves restaurants in places where he knows he will never return, even though he can't hope to boost his reputation that way. He concludes that it is as though he is unconsciously practising being the person he wants to be, as though working up a moral muscle so he won't fail tests in future despite being tempted. Note Frank is still recognizing that being perceived to be a good actor is crucial to flourishing as a social animal, but that often the best and most effective tactic over time is to cultivate the very qualities that you want others to find in you.

A second good answer to queasiness comes from recognizing that everyone is in the same boat. That is not to consider the human condition as malign in pursuit of good impressions, but instead that this is an expression of universal vulnerability. We have in common that no one will have access to our true selves, as if there is any meaningful way to think of such a thing. We are all condemned to partial and to some degree inaccurate perceptions and impressions of us which we must learn to manage.

There is a humility that comes from recognizing that we are all in the same boat when it comes to making an impression. But for all the warnings against the arrogant belief that one is above the fray, let's not fetishize humility either. High self-esteem is good for us much of the time, and while we might celebrate the need for humility as well, we should be aware of drifting into a form of bad faith known today as the humble-brag. C. S. Lewis captured the best of Robert Frank's advice above by noting that humility comes 'not from thinking less of yourself, but from thinking of yourself less'.

The social animal is made out of crooked timber and riven with conflicting needs and worries. And that's not so bad. I asked a friend recently about whether she also felt 'impostor syndrome' at times. She said, 'Of course, everyone does, that's why there's a term for it.' To develop this thought, if you recognize that we are equally fragile in our pursuit of good impressions and a reasonable degree of self-esteem and that we are more dependent on others than we would like to be, we can achieve a deeper level of integrity – the level that recognizes the weakness and frailty of our common humanity and perhaps see this as an invitation to be kinder to each other and ourselves in our pursuit of being judged well.

There is no way to be a social animal without managing impressions and in doing so tracking the impact we have on each other. And yet we can live with integrity too despite this fact. It appears that when we project a version of ourselves we are largely motivated to avoid bad faith and to manage impressions in a way that is congruent with what we believe to be true about ourselves; in line with what psychologists call our self-concept. Yes, we need to act out, but not necessarily to mislead. Technique in this case is a necessary condition of transmitting a reasonably faithful version of a self, because in a social minefield, truth will not win out by itself. And the perceived truth, if persistent enough to hold up over time and across audiences, will, for good or ill, become your reputation.

2

The right kind of reputation

CASSIO   *Reputation, reputation, reputation! O, I have lost my reputation! I have lost the immortal part of myself, and what remains is bestial. My reputation, Iago, my reputation!*

(WILLIAM SHAKESPEARE, THE TRAGEDY OF OTHELLO, THE MOOR OF VENICE, ACT II. SCENE III, 262–9.)

How readily will you acknowledge the importance of your reputation? Not many are as frank as the distraught Cassio. Yet we've just seen the energy, effort and skill people put into conveying the right impression. Reputations are even more demanding than making a good impression since they are impressions that hold up across time and place. Similar to action at a distance, a reputation is something that is assented to by third parties (including people we have never met) rather than direct interlocutors, and it will last – at least until it is lost. Reluctant to feel that the judgement of others is more important than intrinsic worth, we might agree with Iago who replies: 'Reputation is an idle and most false imposition; oft got without merit, and lost without deserving.'

More than twenty years ago, the social psychologist Nick Emler identified reputation management as one of the primary goals of communication. Now that so much talk is visible through social media, we can see and quantify the scale of this effort to be seen as popular, 'like'able, funny, impressive, well intentioned, skilled, interesting and so on. At a time where we are swamped with information, attention becomes the scarce resource.[1] In this context, reputations are crucial for people and organizations if they are to be heard amid the babel of voices. In our amateurish ways we track the metrics of authority, popularity and more. Our inbuilt urge for social comparison can now be supercharged with a never-ending social media window into the lives of others, each of which is presented in the knowledge that others are looking and comparing. Sometimes these comparisons are unflattering and the professionals are here to help, at a price. Michael Fertik, author of *The Reputation Economy* and founder of a company called Reputation.com, offers to clean up your digital act for upwards of $1,000 and has helped over 1.6 million customers put their digital identities in the most favourable light possible. It is not surprising that such services are in demand when, as it is said, surveillance is the business model of the internet and we are only one reckless tweet away from reputational self-immolation.

The reputation economy has become something of a meme in this digital age and applies as strongly to companies as it does to individuals. It can be also be seen as one consequence of the sharing economy. Companies like Getaround and Parking Panda (which enable people to share cars and parking spaces respectively), alongside numerous others like Airbnb and Skillshare, are finding ways to release untapped resources for those in need of them, through sharing. But this brings with it a tight focus on reputation. You might join Airbnb but don't want to have someone in your house that you can't trust. When I book an Uber to drive my daughters home from a social event, I note the driver's score as rated by other passengers. So, in some sense, reputation is more powerful and important today than ever.

Notwithstanding the feverish light into which this need has now been thrust, the truth is we have always needed a good reputation because we have always been susceptible to the judgement of others. Tempting as it is to side with Iago, Cassio is right; we need to be admired and respected. Inconvenient as this may be, without a good reputation we could barely function. Without being judged as trustworthy or impressive in key ways, our chances of living a flourishing life would be seriously diminished. This is because we are enmeshed in a web of social interactions which depend on such perceptions, the reason being that we do not have access to each other except

through 'outward show'. All you have to go on is how I appear
to you. The reality, whatever that is exactly, cannot be directly
accessed.

This is not to deny Iago his point entirely. Reputation-
building is a precarious and contradictory business and often
terribly unfair. We judge each other poorly (as I will explore
in the next chapter) and as a result people acquire reputations
that are damaging to them or potentially misleading to
others. Reputations are so important people make great
efforts to conjure them up often with deceitful intent. As we
will see in this chapter, the distinction is frustratingly hard
to pin down. Ironically, Iago's own reputation as an honest
man was itself 'got without merit' and was key to duping
Othello into believing his wife was unfaithful, with tragic
consequences. You could add that Othello's own concern for
his reputation as an upright and honourable soldier also led
him to his doom. Our ambivalence is understandable. Iago
says 'I am not what I am' (I.1, 65), thus bluntly showing us
the gap between appearance and reality. But the reality thus
revealed is conjured up by the fact there is an audience to hear
his stage whispers. The need to separate appearance from
reality, which runs deep within us, doesn't mean that such a
separation is even possible.

Perhaps our best hope is for a reputation that stands up
over time, remaining consistent with our words and actions,
thus differing from the efforts of obvious manipulators.
Maybe the thing we most dislike in others is the thought of
conscious manipulation rather than the fact that we all need a

reputation. If someone acts in a way that *earns* a good reputation, the queasiness disappears.

Earning a reputation

Every year I attend the Index on Censorship Freedom of Expression awards. Like many awards ceremonies, there is a fair amount of mingling and chatting over drinks before the event, and some consciousness of who has turned up and the general rubbernecking that comes with glitzy events. But when the recipients of the awards are announced for the ceremony itself, the tone changes substantially. We hear stories of people who never thought of this limelight while toiling in obscurity, often at considerable risk to their own safety, for months or years against injustices of various kinds. When they come up for their awards and speak, the atmosphere in the room is reverential. The contrast between the award-winners' huge entitlement to admiration with their apparent lack of interest in courting it is so great as to demolish cynicism. The familiar refrains I overhear (and echo) as the audience walks out are of being humbled, awed, inspired and – in this context, for once – far from cliché and completely apt. Contrast this with Oscar ceremonies, where the setting invites a different response (fairly or not) simply because we know there are public reputations to manage. Highly successful and privileged movie stars dedicating their awards to world peace, social justice and the environment can trigger accusations of 'virtue signalling', which can set off warning bells in the mind of the viewers, who are making an assessment of how seriously to take the stars' performances. W.H. Auden captures something of this ambivalence in his dedication of *The Orators* to his friend Stephen Spender:

> Private faces in public places
> Are wiser and nicer
> Than public faces in private places.

Reputation, if not obviously being sought, is something we rightly cherish and value. And in a case where manipulation is clearly in place (cue sideswipe at politicians), we aren't really denigrating the value of reputation. We are saying that the manipulator has now earned a reputation for social climbing, or showing off, or hypocrisy. If anything, these negative judgements reinforce the value of reputation all the more. If you want a good reputation, you'd better not look too much like you want a good reputation.

But very few people have earned their reputations as convincingly as the Index award-winners. Most of us are working harder than that, sociometers at the ready, and nudging and recasting in search of more flattering light. And because we as performers are prone to self-promotion, we as critical judges have developed excellent bullshit detectors. And we apply these to people whom we have never met, but of whom we develop an 'instinct' about authenticity.

Think of types of reputation that attach to various public figures: Mandela, Churchill, Madonna, Angelina Jolie, Margaret Thatcher, Pope Francis, Donald Trump, Angela Merkel, David

Beckham, Michelle Obama, Taylor Swift. When you think of these people, many adjectives may come to my mind such as dignified, eloquent, talented, brash, flexible, ignorant, driven, pious, intelligent, untrustworthy, generous, witty, friendly, cynical, cruel, brave, charismatic, honest, strong, organized, kind, arrogant. And then think about how fluid the relationship is between these words and these people. Their relationships depend so much on contexts and audiences. The list I might pick for Donald Trump won't be the same list Nigel Farage might pick. The lists go on and so do the range of qualities for which any of us might become known to others to some degree. The list of adjectives above isn't intended to correlate with the list of names particularly well. In fact, it is striking how quickly we can apply a varying range of attributes to a wide range of people. Think of Churchill indomitable in war time versus Churchill losing an election during a post-war peace. While talk can fix a reputation in the mind, the reality is always more complicated and achieved in particular social contexts.

Analysts who try to explain the 'Trump phenomenon' in particular are stymied by the fact that his constant lying, inconsistency and offensive language and behaviour did little to undermine his perceived authenticity in the minds of those who voted for him. The best explanation I've seen as to how this can be comes from the social psychologists Stephen Reicher and Alexander S. Haslam. For them, Trump is able to convey to this group that he is 'one of us', and inculcates commitment from his followers in various ways. First, he uses fairly simple theatrical skills. At rallies, for example, people need to wait for a long time before he turns up. Each person in the crowd will have committed their time, creating a strong sense that this must be something important if they've had to wait so long for it. The same goes for each person's assessments of why others are doing the same. A collective sense of importance emerges. Then, when Trump eventually does turn up, he is quick to identify the concerns of the people in the crowd ('we are being beaten') along with a list of scapegoats who can be blamed for their pain. A strong 'them' can be very helpful in creating a strong 'us'. This is reinforced by a mechanism for identifying the enemy within, for example, the journalists attending the rally or the occasional protestor. If there is any sign of someone protesting in the crowd, the audience are invited to alert security by turning to this enemy and chanting 'Trump, Trump, Trump', giving the people a sense of the power they have to overcome their enemies more generally.

These 'identity festivals' mean the success of Trump rallies owe much to an audience who perform their devotion to Trump, and to an audience and security apparatus who perform as a community under threat. The media are a visible presence, there to be derided and maligned by Trump as the voice of a hostile establishment. The authors cite a journalist who watched the rallies and who describes one such incident:

> Trump scowls at the media cattle pen in the back of the room and calls the press the 'most disgusting' and 'most dishonest' people he's ever seen, pantomiming his disdain

with an elaborate sneer before goading his supporters to turn and glare too. On cue, the crowd turns and boos.

In this moment, the tables are turned. The media and establishment are no longer big and powerful. They are small and cowed by Trump's legions.[2]

The rally becomes a 'lived expression' of Trump supporters' ability to overcome their enemies on a larger scale and contributes to making the hope he offers seem 'real'. Reicher and Haslam describe Trump as an 'entrepreneur of identity' who presents himself as prototypical, as opposed to typical of his audience. He does not hide his money and lifestyle or try to dress down to create a sense of 'us'. Instead, he flaunts his wealth and crudeness to reflect the aspirations of his audience while showing that he 'can't be in this for personal gain'. That is to say, he is aiming to be prototypical of an 'ordinary American' in-group while positioning himself as the very opposite of the typical or prototypical politician who by contrast must be 'crooked' and in it for themselves.

I've described the Trump phenomenon as a way to show that the path to a reputation is not obvious and is created in particular contexts. And while over 61 million people voted for Trump, more than that did not and the loathing and disgust he has cultivated in the minds of those who do not follow him just shows how audience-specific a reputation can be.

While most of us don't need to be concerned by fame or notoriety, we still nevertheless develop in some way reputations that last over time, and these might be discussed by others (friends, family, colleagues) when you aren't there. If most people do not operate on a public stage or have the opportunity or the necessity of impressing crowds at a distance or over time, their reputations are still secured with skill, effort and luck – even if at a smaller scale and with a fixed audience.

When we try to work out what to believe about other people, we are confronted with the fact that they are trying to influence what they would like you to believe. Because they, too, have desires, motives, wishes and wants and we don't all want the same things for each other. To believe what someone is telling you is to have confidence in them akin to believing that a bridge will be solid enough for you to cross it – the only difference is the range of factors you need to consider (because you can be pretty sure the bridge will never want to fool you into believing it is sound). We consequently tread carefully. *Homo sapiens*, 'the knower', should be renamed *Homo credens*, 'the believer'. We need to believe, but we worry about what and who to believe and equally we worry about seeming believable.

Credibility is the currency of social exchange. To have confidence in what you say is to give you credit. If we have credit people trust us and have confidence in us; if we lose it, we have neither. We gain credit and we lose it in light of our words and deeds. And in assessing your credibility, I need to watch out that I'm not being credulous.

It is for this kind of reason that philosopher and social psychologist Rom Harré said that reputations are the single biggest priority in a human life. In his book *Social Being*, he elaborates on this point using the concept of 'character':

An essential element in the understanding of the social activities of human beings derives from their attribution to each other of permanent moral qualities. I have called this attribution 'character'. It is made of the attributes that a particular group of people ascribe to an individual on the basis of the impressions they have formed of him on the basis of his expressive activities. These attributes, or rather the beliefs that people have as to those attributes determine the expectations that a group forms of a person. They are the foundations, as individual beliefs of the willingness of others to defer to and praise an individual or to denigrate him, or simply ignore him. They are the ultimate basis of his moral career.[3]

Harré takes the idea of a 'moral career' from Erving Goffman. Goffman conceived of this idea to describe a person's life according to the judgement of others, in particular, how the life described navigates between the experience of being seen with respect or contempt. The trigger for these judgements comes from how the individual being judged responds to the many hazards put in their way. A hazard is a moment that generates success or failure in the eyes of others and can occur at various points in a life and in different institutional settings. Think of a child taking exams, and the implications this has for her sense of self-worth. Alongside the sense of self-belief or self-doubt that comes with success or failure when confronting a hazard, we need the techniques to ensure that we are still judged well.

A moral career needs to stand up in the eyes of others if it is to be credible over time and place. Given the value of a good reputation, we've learned a set of skills to help manipulate reputations and manage impressions. For instance, we can all avoid being caught in a lie with a host of evasions, exaggerations, distractions, feigning and wishful thinking. And in the pursuit of being judged well, we bend and twist. Honour as we may the true, the good and the beautiful, we will often fall short of those ideals in pursuit of a good reputation. Accordingly, we have ways to test that credibility. In particular, having language enables us to gossip, which is a mechanism through which reputations may rise or fall over a great distance. A look at the most popular forms of social media offers a good reminder of our enormous appetite to produce and consume gossip. And gossip begets gossip. Many social psychologists have identified that an ultra-social species has developed a very deep instinct for reciprocity.[4] This is not just in the conventional form of exchange of goods but this extends to gossip too. Revelations encourage us to reciprocate with revelations of our own. And so on ...

Gossip, for all its harms, can help insure against the cynical conclusion that people are faking their way to good judgement. It is very hard to build a sustainable reputation this way over time because, as Abraham Lincoln is supposed to have said, 'You can't fool all of the people all of the time.' They talk to each other and thereby solve the divide and rule. The boy creates common knowledge by bursting out with 'But the emperor is naked!'

Gossip may be ugly in its own terms but it serves a function. The moral psychologist Jonathan Haidt and colleagues found that gossip is overwhelmingly critical. In their studies they found a ratio of ten reports of transgressions to every one paean of praise, offering that 'gossip is a policeman and a teacher'. As they put it, 'When people pass on high-quality ("juicy") gossip, they feel more powerful, they have a better shared sense of what is right and what's wrong, and they feel more closely connected to their gossip partners.' And in those same studies Jonathan Haidt discovered a double standard in how much people dislike 'gossips' themselves, despite their ubiquity. His ambivalent conclusion is that while gossip and reciprocity might in theory function very well, because each individual doing the gossiping is also motivated by reputation management, they will tweak and twist to enable self-serving bias and hypocrisy.

If we accept the need of a good reputation to flourish, then we still need to unpack what might go into that word 'good'.[5]

Nice and in control: the twin peaks of a good reputation

When we assess a reputation we are making a prediction as to how that person would behave in certain circumstances. But since we are riddled with contradiction, this is not a simple story. Alongside the contexts in which our behaviour might change, looking within, we often have to manage tension and discomfort when our thoughts or behaviours conflict. If I know that drinking can cause seven types of cancer[6] and I carry on drinking this creates cognitive dissonance which threatens my reputation for consistency. This I have to resolve by compartmentalizing or rationalizing my thoughts and behaviour while actively avoiding situations where they obviously come into conflict. The psychologist Leon Festinger discovered this tendency to confabulate when confronted with such contradictions. He studied a cult who predicted that a flood was going to destroy the earth on 21 December 1954. The most committed of them gave up their jobs, relationships, college or sold their homes to commit to the cult completely on the expectation of being rescued by a flying saucer the night before the cataclysm. Of course, on the appointed night there was no visitor from outer space, and subsequently no flood. The members stayed up until dawn in disbelief. The most zealous cult members, faced with this clash between their belief and the evidence on the day, conjured up the idea that it was because of their unwavering faith that the flood had been called off.

But cognitive dissonance arises most sharply under a particular condition which sheds light on the elements of a good reputation. This insight comes from another social psychologist, Eliott Aronson, who made the deep observation that we suffer most when there are threats to our reputation for consistency around either our *motives* or our *competence*. As he put it, we are most inclined to feel dissonance when we feel unable to support the claim that 'I am nice *and* in control'.[7]

Steven Pinker, summing up the literature on cognitive dissonance, comments that it is 'always triggered by blatant evidence that you are not as beneficent and effective as you would like people to think. The urge to reduce it is the urge to get your self-serving story straight'.[8] And the consequent need for a coherent social narrative to describe ourselves over time requires we are able to present a convincing account on both fronts. The social psychologist Susan Fiske and her colleagues have been most recently associated with claiming universal status for this distinction between motives and ability, which she contrasts as 'warmth' versus 'competence':

> According to recent theory and research in social cognition, the warmth dimension captures traits that are related to perceived intent, including friendliness, helpfulness, sincerity, trustworthiness and morality, whereas the competence dimension reflects traits that are related to perceived ability, including intelligence, skill, creativity and efficacy.[9]

In general, she points out, that while we have a slight preference for warmth over competence – limitations on the former, after all, hinder other people, whereas weakness on the latter dimension mainly hinders the self – the most desirable reputations come from achieving both.

In the reputation economy, we need to achieve warmth and competence, popularity and authority, being liked as well as being respected. Which reputation wins out depends on context and what is at stake. In the film *Saving Mr Banks* the main character Pamela 'P.L.' Travers (who would later write *Mary Poppins*) has a difficult upbringing which we see through a series of flashbacks. In particular, she has mixed feelings about her parents. She adores her father but can't help noticing his declining grip on reality, his alcohol-ridden fantasies and his inability to hold down a job. But when her mother attempts to commit suicide as a result of being under so much strain we see the other side of this equation starkly. When she says to Pamela, 'I know you love your father more than me' and tells her to look after the other children, we see the panic on her daughter's face at the thought of being abandoned to a complex world without expert guidance. In Pamela's eyes her father was nice but not in control while her mother was the reverse.

The hit TV series *Breaking Bad* tells many gripping stories, and a key one running through the show brings out this central point about reputation. The series focuses on the transformation of Walter White (played by Bryan Cranston), from a fastidiously upright and gentle person (chemistry teacher, family man) to a feared drugs baron nicknamed Heisenberg (after the Nobel prize-winning physicist), producer of the best meth amphetamine in town. Walter wouldn't run a red light, while Heisenberg would ruthlessly murder anyone he perceives to be a threat. The transformation takes time and has complex counter-currents running throughout. At the start of the series, and the trigger for his transformation, Walter was diagnosed with a lethal lung cancer. His 'breaking bad' was the only way he could think of, using his expertise in chemistry, to support his family financially after his death (as well as to pay for the treatment that might extend his life). Yet despite this overarching narrative, the viewer can see other motives in play which are particularly relevant to this chapter.

Walter is no ordinary chemistry teacher. He was a particularly gifted scientist who had co-founded Gray Matter Technologies with his friend Elliott Schwartz.[10] He and Schwartz fell out over Walter's then-girlfriend Gretchen, who went on to marry Schwartz. The fall-out led Walter to sell his stake in the company for $5,000 and then watch it grow into a multi-billion-dollar enterprise. This is the most acute type of social comparison Walter can suffer. His friend and his ex-girlfriend, now happily married, invite him to lavish parties at their mansion and try to be kind to him. They even offer to pay his huge medical bills when they learn of his diagnosis.

Not only does Walter refuse the offer (pretending to his wife that he has accepted it), he starts to reveal signs of the years of bitterness, humiliation and rage he has, until now, managed to suppress. And it is this set of motives that I'd argue best explains how he is capable of such a sustained transformation. However slippery a slope he is on (as the levels of risk and violence climb alongside the body count), Walter never loses his footing. The programme does a good job of showing the conflict he must endure, his better angels wracked by guilt and panic, his demons keeping him ruthlessly focused and proud of his ability to outwit his many enemies.

And it is these angels and demons we often have to deal with as we manage our reputations. They represent those two axes of a good reputation that often seem overlapping but are in fact conceptually distinct. Walter was nice but Heisenberg was in control.

Why do we need both of these attributes? And how do they come into conflict with each other? A good place to start is to think about what it means to trust someone. Colloquially, when you say you trust somebody it is natural for that to be an assessment of their motives, values or ethics. You trust them not to let you down because you trust their sincere intentions will ensure they do not put other self-serving motives ahead of doing the right thing. This aspect of trust is clearly centrally important to a functioning hyper-social animal, like us. What we recognize less often is that *competence* is equally central to trust. The bridge after all has to be strong enough to hold you up. Your ability to trust me is based on my perceived *morality* and my perceived *capacity* to deliver on my promises.

Not that either of these is a simple concept or easy to determine. But in essence, if I don't trust you to take my money to the bank, it's because I fear you might pocket it (not very nice) or that you might lose it (not in control). In some ways this links back to our discussion of shame and guilt in the last chapter. We can blame someone for a moral failing in a different way to a physical failing because they have more control over the first, and thus can be held more accountable. And we suffer in distinct ways when we fail to achieve these forms of good judgement. If I fail to come across as nice this might trigger guilt. I've transgressed morally in some way. If I fail to be in control, competent, skilled, I am more likely to experience shame, and might feel repelled by my own clumsiness or weakness.

And so it is with Walter, who experienced enormous shame for being the nice guy who came last, while Heisenberg constantly battled guilt as a result of his nefarious and violent transgressions. The sad fact is that we need to choose between the two more than we would like – there are too often cases of people being well motivated but ineffective, and of the reverse. It is hard to be both kind and competent; to be both warm-hearted and cool. The need for status, power, money, sex, self-esteem and so on play havoc with our better angels and risk beginning to turn our Walter Whites into Heisenbergs at any moment. And we make assessments of each other as to the likelihood of those mixed motives coming into play.

What might you distrust if you doubt that I'm well motivated? We can put this on a scale ranging from a lack of interest at one end, through greed, say, all the way to malign intent and wishing me harm. Even if you just want me to look after your cat for the weekend you need to make similar assessments. If you didn't trust my motives for saying yes, you might think me:

1 Lazy – you think I won't bother to feed him.
2 Greedy – I might sell him on eBay.
3 Cruel – I might hurt him.

There are so many ways your motivation and mine are not directly aligned. In fact, the closer we look at it, it's almost certain your wants and mine aren't aligned very much at all. I might be motivated to look after your cat because I'm nosy about seeing your house, or I might be using the excuse to get the key to burgle you, or to have somewhere to invite friends over for a party. I might have a sneaking suspicion that you're not as high-brow as you like to come across and by finding your Mills & Boon collection can confirm that and feel less intimidated when we next meet. And I might not even be fully aware of my own self-discrediting motives. Our capacity for self-deception makes us all the more believable for having convinced ourselves of our good intentions in the first place. The things I end up doing once I'm in your house may well be different from the reasons that led me to agree to help out. The fleeting appetites that can twist our motives vary in intensity in different settings but all add up to reasons why you might not trust me on this dimension.

For you to trust me is take a leap of faith that your motives and mine are sufficiently aligned. But what helps you take this leap? How do I convey my trustworthiness to you?

Since I could just be telling you what you want to hear, your ability to trust me depends on things that I have less control over. Gossip, as we've seen, is a good source of information that I can't so easily control. The same goes for the physical signs that we mean what we say. Steady eye and hand, easy smile, the right amount of emotion: too much and we seem unstable, too little we seem cold. There is much speculation that emotions evolved as guarantors of our sincerity precisely by being hard to control.

What's more, if I tell you things that reduce my competence in a safe way that might help you credit my motives in return, I can seem nicer by giving up some control. If I confess I'm not an early riser and thereby risk not getting the job, I might paradoxically enhance my chance of getting it, because what you need is to have reasons to believe what I'm saying. Sometimes I can gain credit by being willing to discredit less relevant aspects of myself. Therefore to show we are nice often involves revealing the things that we have little control over. How many times do we hear people confess to being 'terrible at this' or 'hopeless at that'. These modest self-deprecations serve to boost up the 'I'm nice' quotient by showing that I'm not too invested in being in control.

Of course, if I go too far with this self-discrediting to show I have nothing to hide and my motives are pure, I can end up discrediting that other key feature of trustworthiness, namely my ability to do the job, my competence. In David Lodge's novel *Changing Places*, academics play a 'humiliation game' in which they gain points for confessing that they had not read well-known works of literature. A young lecturer wins by admitting he has never read *Hamlet*. His refreshing honesty however, while displaying good intentions, reveals too much of a skills gap. This was a conversational malfunction from which he could not recover, and ended up losing him his job as a result.

This takes us to the other side of trustworthiness. It is not enough to be seen to be well-motivated. Competence is crucial, and in many contexts much more important than warmth or being nice. My daughter Ellie describes a science teacher she once had as very likeable but unable to control the class. And she says, all the other children knew this too, pointing out that being in control is even more important than being nice if a teacher is to be respected. And if you are preparing for major surgery would you rather have the surgeon with a wonderful bedside manner but a less than perfect track record, or the slightly narcissistic one with a bit of a god complex, who is famed for being phenomenally skilful? As Montaigne observed:

> The religion of my doctor or my lawyer cannot matter … I scarcely inquire of a lackey whether he is chaste; I try to find out whether he is diligent. And I am not as much afraid of a gambling mule driver as of a weak one, or of a profane barber as of an ignorant one. … For the familiarity of the table I look for wit, not prudence; for the bed, beauty before goodness; in conversation, competence, even without uprightness.[11]

Let's go back to me looking after your cat. If I flaunt my inability to get up in the morning too well, I may in fact lose the job despite having conveyed that I am well-motivated and honest. You need me not only to want to deliver but to be able to deliver if you are going to give me credit. The bridge has to withstand the weight of all that traffic. There are myriad ways I can fail on this dimension and lose the right to look after your cat. You might think I'm:

1 Stupid – too dumb to follow your instructions.
2 Inept – too clumsy to open the tin of cat food.
3 Distracted – going to turn up on the wrong day.

How do you convey to someone that you are skilled? Status markers or reputation conferring mechanisms are constant proxies we use for levels of skill or expertise which we can rely on to some extent. Qualifications are most useful in formal settings so we take care of our CVs. Sometimes credit by association will do the job. If you pay $120k to attend Wharton Business School, when you can watch their lectures for free, you are looking for a few more things than mere instruction. One of those is the reputational benefit that comes by association with a prestigious institution.

In the rarefied atmosphere of academia, people often bemoan the need for prestige. An idealistic insistence that the truth will out and people will get credit on merit alone is belied by the reality. Academics need to establish their credentials if they are to be heard in the first place. They cannot but rely on filters and proxies. Letters after a name, the backing of a prestigious institution, publishing house and journal are all heuristics they need without which their claims would be lost in a babel of undifferentiated voices. And as we've seen with the hapless *Hamlet* non-reader above, they need to maintain an air of competence and expertise in their mode and manner and in what they convey and conceal if they are to be taken seriously.

And as it is in academia so it is in everyday life. We are constantly looking for cues that indicate someone is competent and skilled. We can't know for sure, and so everyone's sociometer needs to be switched on, and not necessarily out of cynicism. A reputation for competence in some settings is tantamount to your right to be heard.

To bring the paradoxical relationship between being nice and being in control full circle, we can often degrade the former to boost the latter. One of the ways I might increase my reputation for competence would be to tone down how nice I am; after all, the whole idea of being able to make 'tough' decisions is predicated on how well you can keep your tender heart in check. Shelley catches this choice in his description of Ozymandias as having a 'sneer of cold command'. More prosaically, when we say someone is 'naughty but nice' or that 'you are awful but I like you', we are showing that credit lost in one department can be made up in the other. We can trade in our moral dubiety for some other excellent feature like charm or wit. And so often, like Walter White, the nice guy needs to work hard to avoid coming last.

We also gain credit for competence, often unfairly, through status and other success signals such as money, power, intelligence, beauty or wit – especially if you are not seen to be striving too hard to make a good impression. A judgement of non-moral excellence can conjure up a feeling of admiration[12] all the more if the feature admired looks like it required no effort. Not surprisingly, people will therefore often conceal the work they've done.

We are confronted by the fact that seeking too obviously to improve a reputation, whether for being nice or for being in control, is self-defeating. The audience is watching and can spot a fake (plastic surgery is still borderline taboo) because everyone knows they want to influence others in this way. And yet we cannot so easily just wish away our attempt to secure good opinion. There's a (possibly apocryphal) story of a lecturer who was teaching a psychology class about positive reinforcement. As she ranged from how Pavlov's dog was trained to expect food on hearing a bell, to what happened when pigeons in a Skinner box were taught to peck for pellets, she didn't notice what the class was up to. The lecturer had a tendency to walk across the front of the lecture hall and back as she spoke, which gave the students an idea. They decided between them that every time she walked to the right of the room they should look uninterested, lean back, whisper to each other, stop taking notes, etc. As she walked to the left of the room that would lean forward, take notes, smile engagingly and one way or another provide her with positive reinforcement. Gradually, she walked less often to the right side of the room and eventually would give the entire lecture from the left corner. The story is funny and poignant. Not only had she been made an unwitting victim of her own lecture topic, she had also inadvertently revealed how much she wanted to make a good impression on her audience.

While some contexts favour motives and morals, and other contexts favour competence and skill, the most prized reputations come from overcoming the inherent tensions between the two.

Trying to do both

I work at an academic publishing company, and when we talk about the reputation we would like our organization to have we use a Venn diagram a bit like in Figure 2.1[13]

This caricatured version of the real thing shows various companies sitting in each of these circles, with differing characteristics as perceived by authors. On the right-hand side you have companies who are perceived as aligned with the authors' values, small enough to give them personal care,

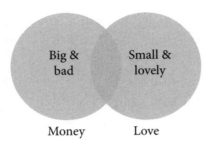

Figure 2.1 *'Money/love' Venn diagram.*

often independent and likely to have a continuity of staff and motivation that the author can rely on over time. Unfortunately, they are not always perceived as the most effective. On the other hand, companies in the left-hand circle are seen as truly effective, with large sales teams and state-of-the-art technology – but not necessarily aligned with the authors as individuals, who are more likely to feel like cogs in a machine. Of course, authors want both. They want the values and alignment and long-term relationships and they also want an effective machine that can bring their ideas to the largest possible readership, along with sales and royalties. In short, they want their publishing company to be nice and in control. This 'Goldilocks' happy medium is an aspiration rather than a reality for any company. In reality companies slide from time to time from one circle to the other, and can rarely sit easily in the middle because tensions continually arise: priorities conflict.

As it is for organizational reputation, so it is for individuals. There is part of us sitting in the right-hand circle with Walter White, and part of us sitting in the left with Heisenberg. And people vary in their tendencies to lean one way or the other. The point however is that the best reputations, for organizations or for people, come from doing both.

Joining	Coaching
Listen, encourage, facilitate	Explain, sell, consult
For people with	For people with
High competence Variable commitment	Some competence Some commitment

Delegating	Telling
Give freedom to decide	Organize, tell what and how, monitor closely
For people with	For people with
High competence High commitment	Low competence High commitment

Figure 2.2 *'Joining, coaching, delegating, telling' matrix (adapted from situational leadership matrix).*

This distinction works at a number of levels. In another work setting, that of manager and managed, we can see these themes emerge again. The literature on 'situational leadership' turns on a distinction between perceptions of people's commitment (being well motivated, etc.) and their competence (being skilled). And the matrix above shows how different engagements are needed depending on where the area of concern lies.

The distinction is there again and when you have someone who can do both, that is, they are high on competence and high on commitment, then you as their manager can feel free to trust

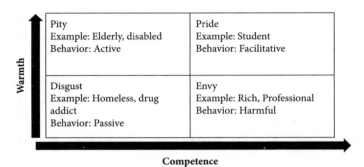

Figure 2.3 *Warmth and competence diagram (modified from the original).*

them fully by delegating. Anything short of that needs a different approach.

Susan Fiske maps out very usefully her dimensions of warmth versus competence in Figure 2.3 by describing how various groups are judged, and which judgemental emotions they elicit as a result of being seen to be high or low on either dimension.

In short, if you are seen as warm but not competent you elicit pity in others who might be motivated to be helpful towards you, if a bit patronizing. If you are seen as competent but not warm you elicit envy and resentment and might incline others to a more hostile stance toward you. If you are perceived as neither warm nor competent you elicit the worst of responses, namely disgust or contempt and the experience of rejection that follows; if you have both (the top right box), you have the strongest of reputations and elicit admiration and pride.

And in TV, films and popular culture we see the twin pillars of a good reputation play out in constant tension with each other.

The choice Walter White made was to give up being nice in return for being in control. His choice is expressed in familiar on-screen phrases like, 'No more mister nice guy' or, 'You won't like me when I'm angry', for example when David Banner turns mean and green as the Incredible Hulk. And by the same token, there are endless on-screen examples of people going the other way, that is, breaking good, where beauty stereotypically tames the beast. In *Pretty Woman*, Richard Gere switches out of corporate raider mode, thanks to the love of a 'pretty woman' (Julia Roberts), and takes his shoes and socks off to feel the grass under his feet before agreeing to be kind and to give up his reputation for being mercilessly cold and successful at the expense of good people.

Of course, in these cinematic and literary transformations we are seeing an oversimplified shift from 'nice' to 'in control' or vice versa. If stories offer idealized transitions of goodies turning into baddies and vice versa, they also offer the function of escape from the more complex turbulence of human traffic. Better art starts to resemble life more closely when mixed motives, compromises, unresolved pain and unfairness are given their due.

Breaking Bad is obviously much less cartoonish than *Pretty Woman* and *The Incredible Hulk* and aspires to a more complex and realistic change of emphasis. The pre-Heisenberg Walter would be judged a nice guy, undoubtedly, but he would also be judged ineffective. He has internalized that judgement too, turning failure into shame and rage. These are enabling circumstances without which the combination of a cancer diagnosis alone would not have led to his life of crime, or at least not for long. Walter Mark II, rebadged as Heisenberg, while protesting throughout that he is doing this for his family (and he no doubt consciously felt that way at the beginning) begins to relish life at the height of his powers. The atavistic thrill he experiences when escaping a dangerous encounter (usually violently), the pride he takes in being the best 'cook' anywhere (his trademark blue crystal meth is of near perfect purity), all indicate that he has found a deep new satisfaction. And even if he knows that people fear him, this is at least a source of huge respect. The pain of his previous humiliations has abated.

It may look as though his breaking bad is breaking free of the constraints of conventional judgement, but Walter is only swapping his audiences around and changing the criteria on which he would rather be judged. I explore the doomed attempt to escape audiences further in Chapter 4. Outwitting the police and making the best methamphetamine only feed his sense of mastery insofar as there are potent audiences who confer that judgement, even if expressed through awe and fear rather than affection or admiration. There were many points along the way that Walter hoped he could hold on to more of Walter Mark I, at least in the eyes of his family. But in the end, he has to forego that hope. In a final conversation with his wife Skyler, he starts to explain why he did all this. She remonstrates, but has misunderstood him:

WALT   Skyler. All the things that I did, you need to
understand —

SKYLER   If I have to hear one more time that you did this
for the family —

WALT   I did it for me. I liked it. I was good at it. And I was really ... I was alive.

Finally, Walt admits what we, the viewers, have seen for a long while. His Heisenberg days may have started out for his family, but he kept going for himself. There were a number of times throughout the series Walt could have quit the business and had enough money to set his family up. But he didn't. With this line, it's almost as if Walt completes his journey from Mr Chips to Scarface while retaining the faintest trace of the recognizably good man that he once was.

But Walter is so addicted to his power that the shreds of 'nice guy' grow too thin for redemption. The drama wouldn't work if they didn't exist at all, if we saw him as a pure psychopath, so the writers have not sugared the story. At least for me, there are enough shreds of niceness remaining that Walter's trail of devastation, which he has brought about (directly or indirectly) temper my judgement of him. That is, to withhold outright condemnation. But I may not feel that way if I were his son, his brother-in-law or indeed many other people watching the very same series. Even for a sympathetic viewer he is not a hero figure that can pull off the elusive balance in the centre of that Venn diagram.

'Heroes'

Of course, we do have a version that achieves this unlikely balance between poles, namely through the 'hero' figure in popular films. The classic trope is as follows: heroes (usually male) don't want any trouble, they just want to get on with their lives and not mess with other people's business. They have a past, of course (which usually credits them with skill and competence), which they might regret or be attempting to escape. They are then provoked by conspicuously bad people who want something from them or to push them around, or most provocatively to hurt someone innocent. This sequence establishes that before whatever is going to follow the protagonist is seen as well-intentioned. But because of outrageous provocation the reluctant hero now has to bring those old skills into play and vanquish the baddies, usually with a level of violence that is proportionate to the harm caused by them in the first place. The film moves us (in the audience) from witnessing someone being nice to being in control, while making sure the nice credentials haven't been lost in the transition. This myth of the hero is the blockbuster film's standard way of showing how to do both. The sequence and context provided enable the shift between the two poles to happen without giving one up, as Walter White had to do.

Of course, writers and directors can conjure up fairly convincing scenes where both dimensions are achievable to persuade a malleable audience. The blockbuster offers its satisfactions but descends into cliché by resolving the tensions too neatly. More complex films offer variants on the pattern, which lean the resulting balance one way or another. The writer is always calibrating for us who are the goodies and the baddies. The sweet spot is achieved when the reluctant hero endures more and more outrage, suppressing his (I'll come back to why it is so often a man) finely honed skills in pursuit of warmth and kindness, only to be pushed too far and then, rather than be a pushover, must flip from nice to in control in a satisfying twist.

The more complex the writing, and therefore the more believable the characters and story, the harder it is to show convincingly how to do both. An example that comes close is the positioning of President Bartlet in a particular scene in another award-winning TV series, *The West Wing*. Throughout many episodes, Bartlet is in conflict with one of his senior advisors, Toby Ziegler. As they approach his re-election, Toby warns the president that he is drifting toward an Uncle Fluffy-type figure, disguising his intellectual superiority (he won a Nobel Prize in Economics) in pursuit of popularity. Not only does he sacrifice his self-respect by playing too nice, it is a losing tactic to compete on grounds of popularity with the much folksier Governor Ritchie, a fictional equivalent of George W. Bush. Toby worries about this and strongly advises that Bartlet doesn't hide his authority under a warm fuzz of goodwill. 'Make this debate about qualified and not', he says.

What is useful about this build-up is that Bartlet's credentials for warmth, or at least a concern for being seen as nice, are established along the way, even as he thinks about bringing out the intellectual big guns. As we approach the one and only pre-election debate, his advisors still don't know which way Bartlet will go, fearing he will fail to be in control either through nerves or by being ingratiating. It opens like this:

GOVERNOR RITCHIE   My view of this is simple: we don't need a Federal Department of Education telling us our children have to learn Esperanto, they have to learn Eskimo poetry. Let the states decide, let the communities decide on health care, on education, on lower taxes, not higher taxes. Now, he's going to throw a big word at you – 'unfunded mandate'. He's going to say if Washington lets the states do it, it's an unfunded mandate. But what he doesn't like is the federal government losing power. But I call it the ingenuity of the American people.

MODERATOR   President Bartlet, you have 60 seconds for a question and an answer.

BARTLET   Well, first of all, let's clear up a couple of things. 'Unfunded mandate' is two words, not one big word. There are times when we're fifty states and there are times when we're one country, and have national needs. And the way I know this is that Florida didn't fight Germany in World War II or establish civil rights. You think states should do the governing wall-to-wall. That's a perfectly valid opinion. But your state of Florida got $12.6 billion in federal money last year – from Nebraskans, and Virginians, and New Yorkers, and Alaskans, with their Eskimo poetry. $12.6 out of a state budget of $50 billion. Now, I'm supposed to be using this time for a question, so here it is: Can we have it back, please?

JOSH LYMAN   Game on!

C.J. CREGG   Oh, my God! [*to Toby*]. It's not going to be Uncle Fluffy.

TOBY ZIEGLER   No.

Bartlett's rejoinder skewers Ritchie with witty panache that unashamedly touts his superior brain power. The satisfaction the viewer gets is of the same type as the hero reluctantly revealing enormous competence. But it wouldn't have worked had the very partisan *West Wing* writers not set Ritchie up for a fall. Ritchie is presented as simple-minded and a potential danger should he get elected, as when he insults Bartlet in an earlier episode and offers, in answer to Bartlet's question on how to tackle rising crime rates, 'Crime, jeez I don't know.' These were provocations meted out on our reluctant hero and allowed Ritchie to be seen as getting what he deserved. But had Bartlet not been nice earlier on, the control would have seemed too harsh. On the other hand, too much fluff would have backfired too. He needed to be able to show his teeth.

But how would the scene have been viewed if the president was Abbey Bartlet rather than her husband Jed? It is hard to imagine this counterfactual context in relation to that scene, to replace the man with a woman, but you can tease this out with experiments. It turns out that while the blend of being nice and control is in tension for most people, and hard for anyone to achieve that intersection in the Venn diagram, that middle way tends to be even less available to women according to some telling research by Frank Flynn and Cameron Anderson using a Harvard Business School study about a successful Silicon Valley venture capitalist named Heidi Roizen. Students were split into two groups. Half were given the original case study, and the other half were given the study but using the name Howard instead of Heidi. This was the only change, so every other detail of the case study was identical. The students were surveyed on their attitudes to the person depicted in the case. The groups found Heidi and Howard equally competent, but Howard was deemed more likeable, genuine and kind while Heidi was seen as aggressive, selfish and power hungry, and not 'the type of person you would want to hire or work for'. It seems that Heidi Roizen faces that double bind of deciding to be a successful entrepreneur or a successful woman, which might have something to do with the hero being, typically, a male figure. It's not within the scope of this book to explore the phenomenon of sexism in detail, but I'll note that when my teenage daughter Anna is asked why she is happy to use the label 'feminist' to describe herself unlike many in her age group, her response is, 'Just look!'.

The fictional world shows how to combine these two dimensions, but the rest of us don't have the luxury of skilful writers and engaged audiences. Our audiences are more fickle and we have to write our own scripts without looking like we are doing so. To have a reputation is something that can depend more on luck than judgement and too naked an attempt to create one can backfire for looking like you're trying too hard. Moreover, the chances we have to manage our reputations are very unevenly distributed and depend on all sorts of prejudicial assumptions. We need to be better intuitive politicians than we like to think if we want to be judged well, because as Jonathan Haidt offers, 'the first rule of life in a dense web of gossip is: Be careful what you do. The second rule is: What you do matters less than what people think you did, so you'd better be able to frame your actions in a positive light.'[14]

This framing is work, sometimes healthy and sometimes humiliating. Celebrities who carry some of their on-screen personae out into the real world are usefully contrasting with most people's experience. Milan Kundera in his novel *Slowness* refers to them as the 'elect'. 'That is where the era founded on the invention of photography comes to the rescue, with its stars, its dancers, its celebrities, whose images, projected on to an enormous screen, can be seen from afar by all, are admired by all, and are to all beyond reach.'[15] The 'elect' are coated in stardust and are in some ways pre-announced. They don't need to explain themselves in quite the same way they would if people had not known them already. They assume an asymmetry of knowledge and significance when walking into most rooms and rarely have to account for themselves or what they do. A friend of mine who works for a charity had a meeting at the house of a celebrity who was a patron of the charity. She was already feeling a sense of vertigo as she went through the palatial home and then she went ahead into the sitting room to discover Naomi Campbell, P. Diddy and George Clooney chatting on the sofa. They paused their conversation to introduce themselves in a courteous but somewhat redundant manner, leaving my friend to introduce herself. A little later when George Clooney made her a cup of coffee and handed it to her, she was quite unable to speak.

Of course, in our digital age the 'elect' are more available to us than ever before. We can see the grain of their lives in unprecedented detail via social media, and often because of their active participation in the swim of communication. Millions will read each day what Kim Kardashian had for breakfast. And yet despite this de-mystification the hunger for them seems undiminished. The queues for autographs when they appear in public are just as long.

The 'elect' are a lucky few, until, that is, they are taken down by the same media who built them up in the first place. The public eye brings rewards but this is a vulnerable place to stand because it has an ambivalent status in the minds of the rest of us watching. On the one hand, we feel the lure and power of fame, and can be star-struck; on the other, some resentment about the unfairness inherent in the lop-sidedness of good fortune.

Psychologists talk about a 'halo effect' that extends from some established strengths to others that are not at all visible. We can see how people attribute characteristics to others with few grounds for doing so. Warren Harding stands as a great example of a US president who failed completely on substantive qualities but was elected because he 'looked presidential', that is, straight out of central casting. Fame, wealth, good looks, being tall and other status markers all generate impressions that invite others to be less critical. A quirky trait might be despised in someone with no power, but seen as eccentric or even charming when exemplified by someone of high status. This is partly to do with the fact that those rich in these gifts have less reason to be accused of using technique to manage impressions. Credibility is attributed more easily to those who conspicuously have no reason to seek it out.

The cruel corollary of all this is that so many features on which most people's reputations hang are quite out of their control, and would be further degraded if they tried too obviously to improve them. This adds to the sense of alienation we can feel when so crudely misrepresented by others who will satisfy themselves with a few blunt cues as to what we may actually be like, and show little interest in looking closer or more carefully. Reputations are unevenly spread and as unequal, unfair and unjustified as inequalities of wealth. They are to some extent dependent on skills, attributes and motives of course, but less than we like to think, and in truth depend somewhat more on luck and timing, and as Iago said, are oft got without merit and lost without deserving. Finally, your reputation only exists in the eyes of your judging audiences and they come with their own preoccupations and peccadilloes.

3

Unreliable judges

The anthropologist Clifford Geertz once said, 'we all begin with the natural equipment to live a thousand kinds of life, and end, in the end, having lived only one'.[1] I had occasion to reflect on this when preparing a speech for my fiftieth birthday party. The reason I remembered this quotation was that, while I couldn't imagine the thousand other lives I could have lived, there was one alter ego I'd been thinking about. His name was Paul. As you saw in the introduction, he first made an appearance in my life at the age of 10, in my first year in a British primary school. We had just moved from Beirut to Purley in south London, and during that first year the teachers decided for a while to call me by my Christian middle name. But Paul vanished soon after that.

Fast forward to 1989 when, after graduating from university, I was attempting to get into publishing and Paul made an unwelcome reappearance. I had written to over a hundred publishers and was ignored or rejected by them all, except for a single interview for a job I didn't get. Talking to my father, he said the problem was my first name and that I should switch to my middle name, Paul. I was shocked at the suggestion, but pretty desperate by then after eight miserable months of applications while working in the jackets, coats and suits merchandising department at Dorothy Perkins. So, I swallowed my pride and did so. Paul did far better than Ziyad had done. He made seven applications and got four interviews.

I still remember vividly sitting in the interview room waiting to be collected after finishing up a pre-interview exercise on a children's encyclopaedia. The interviewer came in and said 'We're ready for you now Paul'. It took me a while to realize he was talking to me, before red-faced and flustering I stood up.

Anyway, Paul was offered the job. At the same time, I received an offer from Sage, the company I still work at today. I'd applied to them previously as Ziyad, in fact, because they were the sole publishers who'd given me an interview in the first batch of a hundred or so applications. So this time around I had reapplied under my first name, assuming they would have me on file.

Faced with two offers, I encountered, in retrospect, a sliding doors moment. We know there are many twists and turns that shape a life but this was one concrete decision I remember that propelled me on a trajectory. Paul went on to work at Kingfisher Books and I went to work at Sage, as Ziyad.

Looking back, I don't know why I was so shocked at my father's suggestion. While publishing might make claims to being a fairly progressive industry, I had seen enough through his eyes, and received enough insights gleaned from a psychology degree, to realize that unconscious bias is rife in human judgements. This is why these days, as part of the effort to combat prejudice, many organizations anonymize the names of applicants to help ensure the employers cannot judge unfairly based on such cues as a non-Western name.

The literature on unconscious bias makes particularly depressing reading when you consider what it tells you about how prone we are to implicit stereotypes and dodgy first impressions. However much we convince ourselves that we are fair minded, evidence suggests we have unconscious biases that colour our perceptions of each other. And because these are unconscious, we have little capacity to do much about it.[2]

Below, in Figure 3.1 we see the results of millions of responses to the Harvard Implicit Association Test.

And while these results are much debated in terms of whether they actually predict racist behaviour at the individual level, in the aggregate they show a pretty disturbing picture. And what we see for skin colour we can see for gender. According to these researchers, we see nurses as women and engineers as men, and much more besides. And this tendency is very widespread. Almost everyone is biased, including members of groups who experience negative appraisals. The concept of 'stereotype threat' is a particularly disturbing finding from a growing body of research which shows how negative stereotypes are internalized by the victims of prejudice themselves. The psychologists Steven Spencer, Claude Steele and Diane Quinn gave a maths test to men and women, telling half the women that the test showed gender differences.[3] The women who were told this did significantly worse than the men, whereas the women who were not given

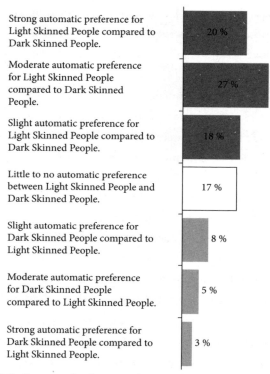

Figure 3.1 *Percent of web respondents with each score.*

that information did equally well. Merely telling women that a maths test does not show gender differences improved their test performance. Similar examples of stereotype threat find that by merely asking people to state their gender or race at the beginning of a test, they do less well, presumably conforming to stereotypes that have thus been made salient.[4] According to Iris Bohnet of Harvard, in the United States, eight billion dollars is spent every year on diversity programs with little evidence that they work.[5]

How we judge – moral tastebuds

Julie and Mark are brother and sister. They are travelling together in France on summer vacation from college. One night they are staying alone in a cabin near the beach. They decide that it would be interesting and fun if they tried making love. At the very least it would be a new experience for each of them. Julie was already taking birth control pills, but Mark uses a condom too, just to be safe. They both enjoy making love, but they decide not to do it again. They keep that night as a special secret, which makes them feel even closer to each other.

What do you think about that? Was it OK for them to make love? (Haidt, 2001, 814).

If you feel it was ok we will return to why this might be. But if, like many, you answered the question, 'No, this was not ok', then ask yourself why you feel that way. Is there a rational explanation for your objection or have you just had a moral flinch? This example teases out the gap between the reasons we think we have for judging and the actual driver of that judgement. After all, Jonathan Haidt and his colleagues have cunningly rebutted, within the description, the obvious objections to do with health concerns for any children, or psychological damage to the sister and brother themselves, etc. In fact, when people who judged that 'Julie' and 'Mark' had done something wrong were asked to give reasons for their reaction they were quickly stumped, yet could not let go of the initial intuition that this was not ok.

Haidt calls this tendency 'moral dumbfounding' and has gone on to explain that when it comes to moral judgements we start with an intuitive response (in this case, yuck!) and then dress it up in logic and reason after the fact.

The psychologist Daniel Kahneman (based on a career of work with his late colleague Amos Tversky) showed that we have two systems of thought that guide our judgement and decision making.[6] System one is rapid, intuitive and unconscious (as when you add 2 + 2, or drive a car while holding a conversation) and system two is slow, explicit and difficult (as when you multiply 247 × 116, or reverse into a small parking space). His point was that much of our thinking uses system one, which is filled with what Kahneman describes as biases and heuristics and fallacies which make us so prone to what he calls cognitive illusions. These tendencies shape our cognitive judgement in myriad ways.[7] The 'availability bias' means we are more likely to think an event will happen if we can easily call to mind an example (such as a news story about a mugging) as compared with using statistical averages. The 'anchoring effect' means we rely too heavily on a particular piece of information when making decisions or estimates. My daughter Ellie was able to demonstrate this with school friends by getting them to guess how old Mahatma Ghandi was when he died. When asked to guess directly they ranged around 80. But when asked to guess after being 'anchored' with a larger number ('was he under 114 when he died?') they ended up guessing an average age of 101 (he was 72). Crafty restauranteurs intuiting this anchoring effect put very expensive wine on the menu to make you feel better about spending more than you otherwise would.

The base rate and conjunction fallacies play havoc with our estimation of relative probabilities. When confronted with a description of 'Linda', a politically engaged philosophy student, and then asked to guess the likelihood that later in life she was 'a bank teller' or 'a bank teller and active in the feminist movement', people chose the latter as more likely. Yet the latter is just a subset of the former and can't be more likely. The list of these biases and heuristics goes on. Meanwhile, system two thinking – more deliberate, effortful, logical and conscious – according to Kahneman, is capable of correcting for errors made in the system one mode.

Kahneman and Tversky were working in the rational, cognitive sphere. But there are parallels to system one thinking that cross from the world of judgement and decision making just described into the sphere of moral and social judgement. For instance, we tend to have an unjustifiably rosy view of both our past behaviour (and anticipated behaviour), while being clearly motivated to forget our own unethical actions. We also use our previous ethical actions to licence unethical action later on (as though drawing on moral credit); we judge whether an action is morally good or bad on the basis of how it is framed, and will often use irrelevant information to judge bad behaviour. We unconsciously favour selfish over selfless interests, without realizing.[8] I'll come back to whether there is an equivalent system two that enables us to correct for these ethical biases.

How often do we respond to daily events and news in our lives and judge them without a rational leg to stand on? We don't like people to be judged unfairly and yet we apply an unusual set of criteria in deciding what is fair. And we have blind spots about our intuitions and hunches. This chapter will explore some of these strange criteria and shed light on the obscure and unusual shape of social judgement.

'Julie' and 'Mark' have entered the literature on moral judgement as an example of how our emotions can lead us down a path to judgement long before our reasoning brain catches up with its post-hoc justifications. The emotion in question here is disgust, and it seems clear from a wide array of research that a flash of disgust can be a powerful shaper of our moral assessments. Psychologists have found this can be very literally exemplified. If you ask a group to wash their hands with soap before answering a questionnaire probing views about issues related to moral purity such as pornography and drug use, their criticisms are more severe than those who had not washed their hands.[9]

Haidt first came across this kind of phenomenon while working with a colleague from Brazil, Silvia Koller. They posed a series of provocative questions to people in both Brazil and the United States. One of the most revealing was, how would you react if a family ate the body of its pet dog, which had been accidentally run over that morning? He found differences between populations in their willingness to judge the story in moral terms. Private school students from Philadelphia found the scenario revolting but would not judge it immoral since no one was harmed. By contrast, different social classes in the United States and people in Brazil did judge the scenario as immoral, drawing on concepts of loyalty, family (the pet was seen as a member of the family), authority, respect and purity.

Our judgement is shot through with normative evaluations. A moral intuition is a suddenly conscious or barely conscious awareness of a reaction to someone else's character or action (like or dislike, yuck or yum, good or bad) – a hot flash of micro-judgement that runs through us often unavailable to inspection by our thinking brains.[10]

While emotions clearly play a role in social assessment, we tend to portray them as clouding our judgement and the choices we make accordingly. Crimes of passion are seen as lesser crimes than those committed in a more calculating mode. And through Philip Roth's painfully insightful description of jealousy as 'the pornography that is a torture to watch',[11] we can see how the profound discomfort this experience can produce can lead to a diminution of responsibility.

But moral psychology states that this is not quite the right picture. While emotions can indeed cloud judgement, the more profound observation is that they *constitute* those very judgements. And this tendency can be seen in various social and legal contexts. From gay marriage through to human cloning, it is pretty clear[12] that disgust plays a part in determining some people's judgements of right and wrong. In the late 1980s actor Ian McKellen was among many campaigning to fight the imposition of Section 28,[13] which prohibited local authorities from 'promoting' homosexuality or 'pretended family relationships'. He ascribed the vehemence of the homophobia driving this change to a revulsion among conservative commentators at picturing gay people having sex.

Leon Kass, who chaired the US President's Council on Bioethics during the era of George Bush Jr, coined the phrase 'the Wisdom of Repugnance' to argue that a tendency to have a 'yuck factor' is a source of deep wisdom in guiding our intuitions about right and wrong:

> Repugnance, here as elsewhere, revolts against the excesses of human willfulness, warning us not to transgress what is unspeakably profound. Indeed, in this age in which everything is held to be permissible so long as it is freely done, in which our given human nature no longer commands respect, in which our bodies are regarded as mere instruments of our autonomous rational wills, repugnance may be the only voice left that speaks up to defend the central core of our humanity. *Shallow are the souls that have forgotten how to shudder.*[14]

Not surprisingly, evolutionary psychologists have speculated that a tendency to feel disgust was a reliable way to prevent us from eating harmful food and spreading disease, and that this has extended into an overdeveloped 'yuk factor', which has further expanded into the moral realm. It is a troubling thought that the aesthetic criteria that helped develop a feeling of revulsion has become part of how we make moral judgements, but as Haidt puts it, 'there's a two way street between our bodies and our righteous minds' (61).

The intriguing claim is that the very source of our judgements is often based on non-rational and unconscious features of human psychology. Haidt's early work (with his incest and dog-eating stories) helped him develop a model[15] to describe how our judgement of others is largely constituted by unconscious processes, which are then dressed up in reasoning and evidence after the fact. We make such judgements when confronted with the stream of stories pouring in through our various screens, while barely conscious of the fact. We may deride the tabloid headlines for labelling those unfortunate enough to be caught in their glare as a 'monster', a 'love rat', a 'national treasure' or a 'hero' as being so simplistic. And yet we are pretty tabloid in our own moral flinches.

Leon Kass and his 'wisdom of repugnance' was understandably berated for these views by many[16] who want to promote a more scientific inquiry free from such 'primitive' reflexes. The contrasting wisdom expressed in Richard Dawkins's letter to his daughter warning her against forming a view based on 'inside feelings' is the very acme of this stance. And, of course, there is great importance in using logic, evidence and argument as much as we can to make our assessments. It's just that we, however wedded in theory to ideals of rationality and objectivity, do so far less easily than we are inclined to admit. And while Kahneman's system two, the more rational and deliberative approach, can correct for errors in reasoning, when the stakes are higher in the social and moral realm we don't seem to have a similar capacity for corrigibility.

I will explore this difference between human psychology and the tribunal of reason throughout this chapter because this is something we should attempt to understand rather than deny if we want to know the basis on which we make judgements of others.

Jonathan Haidt takes these insights much further by exploring how deeply and distinctively our moral instincts depend on quite specific unconscious processes. It seems that the value system that informs social judgement is rooted in a range of moral dimensions which vary for different people. Haidt uses the metaphor of tastebuds on the tongue to describe these moral tastes. In the same way that our tongues enable five taste perceptions (salty, sour, bitter, sweet and savoury), in the case of our righteous minds (as he calls them) we also have taste receptors, or more properly, moral foundations. These are:

1 **Care vs harm.** This foundation relates to the impulse to be kind and to avoid pain to others. It leads us to believe that hurting people is wrong and that caring is a moral good. This foundation drives us to judge someone as cruel or callous on the one hand, or kind, caring and compassionate on the other.

2 **Fairness vs cheating.** This foundation is about justice, fairness, rights and autonomy and the dislike of cheating. People have rights that need to be upheld and justice requires a proportional response to infractions. This might lead to judging someone as dishonest and greedy or as fair-minded and reasonable.

3 **Loyalty vs betrayal.** This foundation offers sacrifice to the group as a virtue. It values loyalty and allegiance, warns against threats from outside the group and punishes

betrayal. This might drive a judgement of someone as selfish versus someone as self-sacrificing and community-minded.

4   **Authority vs subversion.** This foundation invites deference to traditions, institutions and authority, recognizing the value of a social order. It punishes those who undermine social hierarchy and celebrates those who show propriety and respect.

5   **Sanctity vs degradation.** This is the foundation relating to the discussion above around how disgust can trigger a moral evaluation. It venerates health, cleanliness and purity (and, relatedly, chastity and piety) and tends to punish sins of pollution, contamination and related traits such as lust and greed.[17] This foundation might lead to judging someone as disgusting on the one hand or wholesome on the other.

'Julie' and 'Mark' infringe on this fifth foundation and therefore generate a negative moral judgement in those who value it highly. People who take their shoes off before entering their own or others' homes or sacred places are obeying the same foundation.[18]

Those who rely on the full range of moral foundations argue that relationships need to be regulated by more than just the first two foundations to create a better bounded and structured social world without which you end up with an irresponsible and chaotic public space. This latter group represent the vast majority of the human population. While most people in most places and times draw on all five foundations there is an unusual group who claim to focus only on the first two 'care/harm' and 'fairness/equality' – people like me and many of you reading, no doubt. We are the ones who claim to refuse to judge 'Julie' and 'Mark' negatively.

This group represents a much-analyzed sub-group known in psychology circles as the WEIRDs.[19] WEIRDs are the minority who live in Western, Educated, Industrialized, Rich Democracies. WEIRDs claim they don't mind the family eating their pet dog, or siblings having sex as long as no one gets hurt, because they claim to lean unusually on the first two foundations, while most people draw on all five. While all humans worry about care versus harm or fairness versus cheating, only the non-WEIRD majority across times and cultures care about authority, loyalty and purity just as much. Social conservatives, even those living in the rich West, seem to have all five moral tastebuds strongly activated.[20]

Nearly half a million people have been tested with scenarios that bring out these differential preferences and the results go a long way to explaining the 'culture wars' in the United States between 'liberal' and 'conservative' political hues, as the political divide tends to be labelled. One scenario depicts a woman who is looking for a cloth to clean her house, finds an American flag, and tears it up for rags to clean out her toilet. When asked to judge whether these scenarios are immoral there is a continuum of responses which correlate the more liberal you are with your likelihood of answering 'no' and the more conservative correlating with likelihood of answering 'yes'. The claim is that these scenarios fall foul of the sanctity, loyalty or authority foundations which are more salient for conservatives and less so for liberals.

There are many reactions to Haidt's compelling contrast of the WEIRD two-tastebud view as against most other people who use all of them. One claim is to say that the two-tastebud view is the best and that progress in the world comes from making the foundations related to community and sanctity redundant. It says that social progress has made us less negatively judgemental and that this is due to this shift. Meanwhile others, like Haidt himself, believe that we need to have the 'yin and the yang' of the liberal progressive and the orthodox traditional in order to keep society on track. The culture wars that flow from such divergent

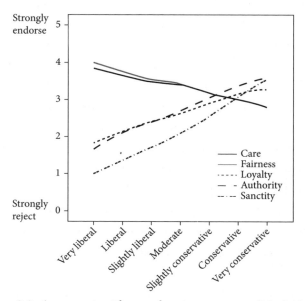

Figure 3.2 *Agreement with moral statements vs political identity (from Haidt, 2012).*

moral intuitions lead to accusation and counter-accusation, with liberals and conservatives lambasted as irresponsible destroyers of the social fabric or rigid oppressors of freedom respectively.

But liberal progressive WEIRDs who claim only to be influenced by the first two principles of harm and fairness could be less 'enlightened' than they think. It doesn't take much to activate the other moral foundations in them too. We may make much of our rational capacities when answering a questionnaire, but when we get close to things we care about, we sound just like anyone else, and will draw on authority, loyalty and purity in various ways.

The tone of the opprobrium that environmental activist and journalist George Monbiot received after deciding to switch toward supporting nuclear power from fellow enlightened environmentalists seems to focus on betrayals of loyalty and sanctity as much as anything else. The environmentalist Jonathan Porritt commented on 'how bedazzled he [Monbiot] now is by "*the promise of integral fast reactors and liquid fluoride thorium reactors*" ... don't they just sound absolutely amazing! Try saying that out loud to see if you too feel a little frisson of sub-sexual arousal!'[21] And journalist John Pilger: 'Chef Monbiot is a curiously sad figure. All those years of noble green crusading now dashed by his Damascene conversion to nuclear power's poisonous devastations and his demonstrable need for establishment recognition – a recognition which, ironically, he already enjoyed.'[22]

There are clubs in all cultures that require loyalty and punish betrayal. The WEIRD preference is to assume others are befuddled by fuzzy self-serving thinking while we (whichever we) are the ones who see straight. Let's not get comfortable with that complacent view, lest we fall into the trap of self-exculpation. This lack of self-awareness is endemic across human psychology and means that the way we judge ourselves is often as distorting as the ways we judge each other. The right-wing commentator James Dellingpole, commenting with delight on the Monbiot fracas, reproduces the same false illusion of rationality, but this time from a right-wing view:

> Empiricism, that's the thing. Things are either true or they're not true. And if they're not true it is clearly wrong to go on believing in them for the sake of ideological correctness. That's what Lefties are doing all the time and, as you've rightly seen in this case, George – though sadly not yet on the issue of, ahem, 'Climate Change' – it's pernicious, corrupting and morally reprehensible.[23]

The picture emerging from psychological research is that, if anything, we need to be wary of a self-image that suggests our judgements are neutral or fair-minded. There is something human about our judgements being shaped by emotion and unconscious processes of self-justification. And, relatedly, we have other processes shaping us just as profoundly. Just as significant as our internal processes is the fact that our identities are socially constituted in such a way that we cannot but see the world in terms of group membership and social contexts.

Judgement in context

Recent political turmoils have made explicit the world of 'post-truth' and 'alternative facts' in which we find the evidence that suits our stances, rather than seeking out the truth. But this kind of 'motivated reasoning' has been with us all along. If you show people footage of a protesting crowd demonstrating outside a building people they will see different things depending on what they learn the demonstration is about. If told they are watching gay rights protestors outside an army recruitment office versus anti-abortionists outside an abortion clinic their viewpoint, and reports on what is actually going on, will often be shaped by political loyalties.

We are often unaware of these social forces, preferring to think of ourselves as more immune to external factors than we are. The fundamental attribution error (as it is known) is a description offered by psychologists of how we ignore context when evaluating why people do the things that they do. If someone gives money to someone in need they do so 'because' they are kind; if someone steals something it is because they are dishonest. It takes research to show that these behaviours happen in a context that strongly affects whether you steal or donate. For example, it turns out that for students at a theological seminary in Princeton, the biggest predictor of whether they would help an injured stranger blocking their path depended mainly on whether or not they were in a hurry. The students in question were given the task of crossing campus to prepare a talk on the story of the Good Samaritan. Along the way they each encountered a man slumped in a doorway moaning and coughing. The likelihood of their helping the man depended mainly on whether they were told they were late or had plenty of time. Some of those in a hurry literally stepped over the man's prone body to get to the next building![24]

Rather than see the power of context, we tend to essentialize qualities in each other, and are shocked when people then act 'out of character'. We tend to overestimate how much choice goes into people's life outcomes, and how little luck, this can lead to a 'just worlds' phenomenon which proposes that people on the whole get what they deserve. People, for instance, tend to believe (in the spirit of the 'American dream') that there is more social mobility and less inequality than occurs in the societies in which they live.[25] I will return to 'moral luck' later in this chapter.

We very rarely make judgements of others in the abstract, except perhaps while filling out questionnaires. Our willingness to judge each other is shaped especially by the relationships we have to each other, and the groups we belong to. The psychologist Solomon Asch spent his career demonstrating how easily we are influenced by the presence of others in making judgements. Even the most elementary perceptual judgements of how long a line is can be distorted by hearing other people say things that fly in the face of the obvious. Look at the image below (Figure 3.3), for example.

Which of the lines on the right is of equal height to the one on the left? The obvious answer is C, isn't it? But if you heard seven other people each answer B how easily would you stick with your view when it came to your turn to answer? It turns out that 75 per cent of students asked would conform with the group

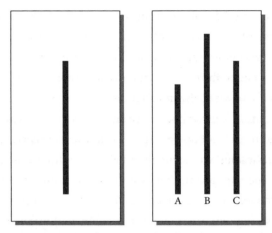

Figure 3.3 *Perceptual judgements – line length test.*

(who were confederates faking it for the instructor) and choose the wrong answer at least once.

The history of social psychology is littered with examples of how our judgements so strongly depend on relationships, group membership or social context. Much of this work was motivated by a need to understand how the Holocaust was possible in a modern society. The names Stanley Milgram and Philip Zimbardo, are well known enough to conjure up images of obedient subjects electrocuting people on instruction from a man in a white coat, or of students too vigorously taking on their roles as guards and students in the Stanford prison study. Psychological concepts like the bystander effect and social proof[26] show how prone we are to acting in accordance with norms implied by the presence of others.

Psychology has shown repeatedly how deeply permeated each of us is by a social identity. This is an important corrective to our illusory self-image as atomized individuals and gives a better insight into our social natures than more everyday intuitions can typically manage. And is why we can't truly understand ourselves, never mind expect other people to understand us. It appears that even the thinnest sense of group affiliations will strongly affect our willingness to judge and act one way or another. The minimal group experiments completed by Henri Tajfel in the 1970s showed groups of boys quickly siding with their own (after being split into two groups at random) at the expense of the other group of boys on the most minimal of criteria. They were divided into two groups based arbitrarily on the names of two painters they had never heard of: Paul Klee and Wassily Kandinsky. When apportioning money or points between groups they opted to take less for their own group if it meant depriving the other group all the more. This minimal condition was supposed to be the control condition against which to compare stronger boundaries, and yet it became clear that a category this basic and meaningless was enough to create in-group favouritism. This is not to say in general that identifying with one group leads necessarily to discriminating against other groups as in the minimal conditions above. That is, distinguishing does not necessarily entail demonizing. If you see yourself as part of a group and want to make your group distinctive it might well be through acting pro-socially toward others, as when people in certain groups decide to help those 'less fortunate than themselves'.

The point simply is that our social identities and the groups we belong to are profoundly influential with regard to how we judge others, for good or for ill.

Our proneness to affiliate with people who we identify with has led persuaders of various stripes to appeal to this tendency. Hotels wanting their guests to think of the environment (and the hotel's profits) before throwing towels out to be washed have found the most effective message they can use is one setting out how other people (especially people like *you* – e.g. people who previously stayed in the same room) reuse their towels too. The behavioural insights unit working with the UK Government on how to increase payment of tax found that a simple 'nudge' could make a big difference. It found that replacing the sentence, 'Nine out of ten people in the UK pay their tax on time' with, 'The great majority of people in [the taxpayer's local area] pay their tax on time' increased the proportion of people who paid their income tax before the deadline.

It's easy to think that this all means we are mindlessly in hock to groupthink and following the herd. But that's not right; we are the opposite of mindless in that we are assessing which groups represent us before allowing their norms to govern our behaviour. We are not hypnotized or made irrational in groups (as often characterized by the tabloid press and in common-sense assumptions about mindless mobs). Rather we ultra-social animals are minded to act in the ways we do because the group norms are something we have signed up for. The social psychologist Mark Levine and colleagues looked at when British football fans were willing to help an injured fan of the opposing team.[27] They found that if the subjects thought in terms of being supporters of Manchester United they would not be inclined to help a Liverpool fan, but if they were put in the category of football fans generally they would stop and help. If, however, the person on the floor was not identifiable as a football fan they were less likely to help again. When we think of football thuggery, it is easy to picture 'mindless' violence where people are reduced to unthinking automatons joining the herd. Far from being mindless, the people in this study are shown to be highly conscious – depending on which group they see themselves as belonging to.

It is important to understand this because it resists the idea that we are sleepwalking into moral judgements or are brainwashed by charismatic leaders. More typically, we are choosing the groups that form our social identities and then knowingly judging within the norms that follow that choice. The norms that govern our faith in institutions massively shape the way we behave and what we consider to be unethical. There is no point standing patiently in line while everyone else has rushed to the front of the queue.

The key point here is that social identities can change and, as they do, the logic of who is seen as 'one of us' changes too. My sense of myself as a father, a publisher, a Londoner, a writer or as someone with Arabic heritage and family shapes the decision space around what it is reasonable for me to think and do quite profoundly. My allegiances, self-esteem, prejudices, willingness to be led or influenced, sense of fairness, sense of solidarity, biases about 'people like me', my judgements all are to an extent shaped by the collective self that is salient to me at the time. This is not to deny my individuality; it is to recognize how it is irreducibly expressed through a social lens, and that my social identity changes the way it makes sense for me to engage with the world. It also creates the disorienting thought that there isn't a singular, essential me for anyone to judge, correctly or otherwise.

The groups we create through social categories influence the types of relationships we form, amplify norms and affect how we evaluate the moral content of our actions. And this affects moral judgements of what is permissible. For instance, in one study college students were asked to solve maths problems with others around but they could cheat by faking how they did and cheating their way to a reward. Some participants were in the presence of a confederate who cheated blatantly by finishing the problems impossibly quickly and leaving the room with the maximum amount of money. This shaped behaviour in a distinctive way. Cheating by others in the room increased when the ostentatious cheater was clearly an in-group member (a member of the same university as the participants) and decreased when he was an out-group member (a student at a rival university).[28]

Yet we are inclined to a Manichean division of the world into good and evil and attribute the latter to explain terrible acts. Our perceptions of light and dark are shaped strongly by the groups we consider ourselves to be part of or which represent us and can relegate those in outgroups to something less or something worse with alacrity. At the most extreme, the other is judged as worthless, irrational or evil. But the myth of pure evil ignores the fact that those acts are committed by people with reasons, and more disturbingly those reasons often sounded (however self-deceptively) high-minded. People don't tend to think of themselves as evil.

When psychologist Roy Baumeister analysed reasons for committing violence, he concluded that greed and sadism only accounted for a small percentage. More disturbingly, the more common antecedents of violent action according to him were high self-esteem and moral idealism. Anyone who watches and winces at the brooding menace that is Joe Pesci as a trigger-happy mafia mobster in various films would be perverse in their assumption that he suffers from low self-esteem. The bully is not always a coward, even if he is vigilant at policing threats to his ego. Baumeister's unexpected conclusion is that some reform programmes that work to build up self-esteem could be self-defeating because they may be encouraging the kind of narcissistic self-regard that can trigger a violent reaction when flouted or defied or insulted. The honour code and ideological commitment are responsible for far greater numbers of violent acts than anything else.[29]

Similarly, ideological purity or idealism can be dangerous in their assumption that the end justifies the means, thereby licensing torture, extrajudicial killings and so forth for the sake of the cause – particularly dangerous with the power of the state behind such idealism.[30]

It is said that history is written by the victors. It is also written by those victors in a particular, neutral sounding way, a tone that would not be used by their victims. Steven Pinker describes this 'moralization gap' as the asymmetry that exists between a perpetrator's world-view as contrasted with that of the victim. The victim has a long memory, while the perpetrator resides firmly in the present; the victim plays the moralist, defining the relevant struggle as between good and evil, while the perpetrator presents as the scientist in pursuit of reasons and extenuating circumstances.

This matters because when we see ourselves purely as rational, individual actors we miss the fact that the social is not just providing the context in which we act. It is deeply constitutive of who we are. But if we to turn to a collective view and merely see irrational action, whether 'mad' rioters, 'crazy' extremists or 'evil' people who have different ideological commitments to our own, then we are condemned to judging others without any chance of comprehending them. A better understanding of our truly social identities would equip us not only with the tools to understand better those who we might ordinarily dismiss as irrational, but also to help us to better understand our ultra-social selves.

The picture emerging from psychological research is that we need to be wary of our self-image as neutral, independent or fair-minded. Not only do we judge each other in ways that are unconscious, moralizing and framed through our social identities, we also have a hard time separating intention from mere circumstances when judging actions.

Moral luck

That the world judges by the event, and not by the design, has been in all ages the complaint and is the great discouragement of virtue.

(ADAM SMITH)

In November 1984, during the bitterest of industrial disputes in modern British history, David Wilkie, a Welsh taxi driver, was driving David Williams, a non-striking miner, to Merthyr Vale colliery. He had just turned on to the A465 north of Rhymney when two striking miners, Dean Hancock and Russell Shankland, heaved a forty-six-pound concrete block off a road bridge. The block hit Wilkie's cab, killing him instantly and slightly injuring Williams, the non-striking miner.

Did Hancock and Shankland thereby murder Wilkie? The court said they did. They stood trial and were found guilty of murder in May 1986 and were sentenced to life imprisonment, despite claiming they only wanted to frighten Williams. This verdict caused an outcry so strong that even though the miners' strike had ended by then, 700 miners walked out of Merthyr Vale colliery in protest. They felt the death of Wilkie was clearly not a deliberate act and were outraged by such a harsh judgement.

Whether they committed murder or a lesser crime depends to some extent on what their intent was. A verdict of murder depends on the state of mind of the perpetrator, both in law and in common sense. Did they have the requisite *mens rea* (Latin for 'guilty minds')? In English law intention is not a simple category. Obviously pre-meditated murder, where you can show the killers had 'direct intent' to cause the outcome, qualifies for a verdict of murder. But there is a weaker version of intent that can also bring about the same judgement. And this was a broad enough category to damn Hancock and Shankland. To qualify as murder in this case it was enough to show that the defendants had 'oblique intent' meaning they had the *foresight* to know that death was a very likely consequence of their actions (even if they didn't desire that outcome). Even if the result was on some level undeserved, the known risk of causing death by their actions was so high that they deserved to be found guilty.

But imagine that the concrete block had landed (as the miners protested was their plan) on to the road, merely causing traffic to be delayed. In that case, they would have received a much smaller sentence, even though they had exactly the same intentions. Without the outcome of someone's death, they could only have been prosecuted for attempt, however murderous the intent.

By separating outcome from intent we encounter the somewhat baffling fact of 'moral luck'. It sounds oxymoronic, but the philosopher Bernard Williams, who coined the phrase, came to realize that we just do judge each other morally for things that lie outside our control. And thus a would-be murderer who by pure chance fails to kill (say, because the intended victim trips just as the bullet whizzes by) is judged less harshly than the one who succeeds despite their having the same intentions and actions. And the reverse is true; it seems reasonable to treat me differently if I do something reckless like throw a brick over a wall depending on the outcome. If it lands harmlessly on the grass on the other side, then I might expect censure for my recklessness but I wouldn't expect to be punished. If instead the brick hit and killed a child, then I would be appearing in court to face a much harsher reckoning.

The film director Luis Buñuel played with this idea in his film *The Criminal Life of Archibaldo de la Cruz* in which a would-be serial killer attempts to murder people who end up dying at the same time, through some accident, despite his failed attempts to murder them. In court the judge finds Archibaldo innocent of all these crimes despite his confession of his intent and deep feelings of guilt. He hadn't caused the deaths he had planned and so there was nothing to punish.

Judging by outcome rather than intent somehow runs against our intuitions about culpability; hence the outrage of the miners of Merthyr Vale colliery in light of such rough justice. And, indeed, later on the case went to the Court of Appeal and the verdict was downgraded to manslaughter.[31]

Clearly both outcomes and intentions matter but in different ways. Moving away from the law into the realm of our deep-seated intuitions, we can see strange features in our capacity to judge beginning to emerge. Our two-system approach to judgement makes another kind of appearance. It seems the more automatic and unconscious system one approach inclines us to focus on outcomes more than intentions. Someone steps on your foot and you react negatively, reflexively, irrespective of whether they meant to hurt you. The second type of judgement, system two, is the more reflective and this focuses on your sense of what was intended, which can in turn modify the first, more automatic reflex.

The developmental psychologist Jean Piaget discovered that young children do not recognize intentions until the age of five or so. There are many experiments that show children seem to lack what's known as a 'theory of mind' at that young age. That is, they struggle to picture how another mind sees things from a point of view that is not their own. Until then they only have the system one reflex to punish outcomes. This means they judge accidental harm as severely as intended harm. Only later do they develop the system two know-how to interpret other minds and the intentions they may have, and thus have the option to put harmful outcomes in context.

But that automatic urge to punish never fully goes away despite our skill at rationalizing. It runs very deep. The speculation is that there was an evolutionary advantage or at least a necessity for teaching children by punishing them irrespective of whether their infractions were accidental or intended. If the child spills the milk, give her a smack, which will teach her a lesson, whether or not it was an accident, especially if the parent lacks the language to explain that spilling milk is a bad thing. We learn best when punished for outcomes, it seems.[32]

When we learn to realise that other people think differently, we can begin to see things from their perspective and as we become adults we learn to balance that first gut-feeling response with the more considered assessments of intention. But moral luck and that original gut-feeling persist. Even when someone has done something terrible by accident, we will expect them to punish themselves with guilt rather than blithely forgive themselves simply on the grounds that the harm was accidental. Even if they cannot, strictly speaking, be blamed for accidentally causing harm they suffer what Williams called 'agentic regret' because they can't deny they were, after all, the cause.

The people who aren't capable of this are psychopaths. Interestingly, psychopaths are much more forgiving of accidents. Undistracted by a gut-feeling system one reflex, they make a colder and more calculating system two assessment of risks. They seem to have a clear understanding of intention and weigh that component heavily without feeling the empathic pain of the harmful outcome that can lead us to want to punish accidental harm.

It may well be that on some philosophical level psychopaths are technically better, that is, more rational judges, than the rest of us because they are more forgiving of accidents (however harmful). They don't mind the ensuing harm and damage that flows from a bad mistake as long as it is clear there was no intent to cause that harm. The rest of us are flooded with the pain of the consequence to such an extent that we can't help but let that affect our sense of what is the right punishment – even if unfairly.

While system one tends to focus on outcomes and system two on intentions, it seems we can take an outcome and use that to distort our perceptions of intention. The unreliability takes a particular form in that we will allow our judgement of the morality of the outcome to affect our willingness to attribute intentionality in the first place. In short, if we don't like what the person did we are more likely to feel they did it on purpose. Take this example from the experimental philosopher Joshua Knobe. He approached passers-by in a park with the following two stories:

The vice-president of a company went to the chairman of the board and said, 'We are thinking of starting a new program. It will help us increase profits, but it will also **harm** the environment.' The chairman of the board answered, 'I don't care at all about **harming** the environment. I just want to make as much profit as I can. Let's start the new program.' They started the new program. Sure enough, the environment was **harmed**.

The vice-president of a company went to the chairman of the board and said, 'We are thinking of starting a new program. It will help us increase profits, and it will also **help** the environment.' The chairman of the board answered, 'I don't care at all about **helping** the environment. I just want to make as much profit as I can. Let's start the new program.' They started the new program. Sure enough, the environment was **helped**.

The question Knobe asked the passers-by was 'Did the CEO intentionally harm the environment?' It turns out that 82 per cent said he did. But when those who read the second story were asked whether the CEO intentionally helped the environment only 23 per cent said yes. The stories are identical except that every instance of 'harming' in the first scenario was replaced with 'helping' in the second, yet the judgement of intent shifted to a remarkable to degree.[33]

This asymmetry in responses, now known as the Knobe effect (or sometimes the 'side-effect effect'), shows that we tie our assessment of something factual, the CEO's intentions, with something value-laden, namely whether the outcome was harmful or helpful. This blending of facts and values – which as the Scottish Enlightenment philosopher David Hume has warned us should have, logically speaking, nothing to do with each other; you can't get an 'ought' from an 'is' – seems to be another quirk of human judgement.[34]

Things get even messier when you consider how we judge each other in the context of differing kinds of harms caused. The tendency to blur intention and outcome itself varies. One distinction that is revealing is where the behaviour being judged breaches moral norms to do with harm, versus moral norms to do with purity. When the harm principle is violated, it matters a lot to know whether the action was intended or not. If it was accidental, it is much more easily forgiven. Yet when the purity taboo is violated it doesn't seem to make much difference whether it was intended or not. We react as negatively to someone farting at the dinner table whether or not it was accidental (this seems to be something to do with that inherited disgust reflex, which may have stood us in good stead in avoiding pollutants). Knowing whether the harm is deliberately intended has implications for whether we avoid or trust the person who did it. There is an echo here of the discussion of guilt and shame in the last two chapters. Guilt is associated with agency and shame less so. Breaking harm norms is associated with guilt and naturally triggers a hunt for the motive; breaking purity norms is the kind of sin that appears to be seen as built into the sinner.

This quick survey of the vagaries of good judgement should again give us pause. There is a gap between our self-image as rational and dispassionate and our actual capacity to judge each other fairly.

Can we judge fairly?

Alan Alda played the character Hawkeye Pierce in the long-running television series *M*A*S*H* which focused on the lives of American doctors in the Korean war. Hawkeye was the central figure of the show who was part hero, part anti-establishment wit. Along with his close friend BJ Hunnicutt, he provides a satirical running commentary on the craziness of life in a war zone. But toward the end of the series something goes very wrong for Hawkeye and his near constant tap of irony and sarcasm dries up to be replaced by darker themes threatening his very mental health. There is a painfully revealing scene that draws out our two-system thinking approach to moral judgement very well. We learn about it through Hawkeye's therapy sessions. He is talking about being on a bus with a woman transporting a loudly clucking chicken. There is great danger to them all but the chicken won't stop clucking. Hawkeye tells her to shut it up, so in her desperation the woman suffocates the bird. Only as we see Hawkeye's ongoing therapy and how dreadfully disturbed he is by the episode do we begin to realize what really happened. His psychological defences collapse and he is forced to recreate the memory and the part he plays, because it wasn't a chicken that the woman suffocated to save them all. It was her baby. Hawkeye's unbearable dilemma confronts us very powerfully.

How could anyone judge the rights and wrongs in a situation like this? It is clear that Hawkeye can rationalize that the outcome led to lives being saved, but it is equally clear that he cannot forgive himself.

The terrible dilemma comes from the inherent tension between system one and system two judgements. The first is the emotional reaction (don't hurt the child) which focuses on doing what feels right irrespective of the outcome versus the second utilitarian view of doing what is right (save the group) based on the impact your actions have on the well-being of others. Can we find a way through these two views to enable better judgements? The philosopher Joshua Greene believes we sometimes can. He recognizes that these two systems are actually embedded in our brains and sit in deep tension with each other. In his book *Moral Tribes*, he uses the metaphor of a camera with in-built settings that enable us to take good photos in many circumstances (an analogy with system one thinking) but contrasts this with the system two–like manual mode that we use for certain conditions that aren't well catered for by the automatic mode (lighting, motion, etc.). This 'dual process' capacity for moral judgement gives us some hope of doing it better than we normally do.

The power of this analogy becomes clear when you see the moral intuitions as the 'automatic settings' that enable us to cooperate to a large degree in many circumstances. Greene's view is that we evolved these to solve the 'me' vs 'us' problem, that is, how we get to move from individual selfishness to cooperation with others. This shift enables us to gain the benefits of cooperation, through developing system one–like social emotions that are triggered fairly automatically such as guilt, love, shame and so on to offset a tendency to be too narrowly self-serving. However, these enable us to be cooperative only *within* our moral tribes. When tribes with differing values meet, we can't rely on those emotional intuitions to see the bigger picture. This 'us' vs 'them' problem does not get solved by how we feel in the automatic mode. On the other hand, he says, we can think our way, in manual system two mode, to solving those problems by using the logical principles of utilitarianism.

Greene's point is that modern life has brought about more frequent conditions under which these system one moral intuitions just won't do in supporting moral judgements in the world. Specifically, he points out that in a world where we are operating across vast distances and populations our instinctive intuitions lead us astray. These automatic settings, our moral tastebuds, can override selfish impulses with more group-oriented ones and rooted in moral emotions like guilt or a need for a good reputation. This is all very well for communities within the scope of anthropologist Robin Dunbar's limit of 150 people, but we now have to solve a different moral problem, namely in moving from 'us' to recognizing 'them'. And 'they' might not be within reach of our intuitive imaginations and capacity for empathy. Here Greene feels we need the more system two like manual mode offered to us by Jeremy Bentham and the utilitarian tradition, one that values all lives equally even if you don't have the same sentimental attachment to strangers that you do to relatives and friends.

While Greene acknowledges Jonathan Haidt's intuitionist model, that we judge first and rationalize later, he also suggests the more deliberative rational mode can and should override that judgement at times. In this more careful system two mode, many can start to see 'Mark' and 'Julie' in a better light than they did at first. Greene gave students their story and then good or bad reasons to justify why it was reasonable for them to have sex. A good reason involved saying that our reaction against the story is an evolutionary overhang which may have served us once in creating an incest taboo, while the bad reason for justifying 'Julie' and 'Mark' was to say that it would create 'more love in the world'. The contrasting rationales made no difference to the initial yuk reaction, the moral flinch, that many had. But after two minutes those who had heard the good reasons were more willing to forgive.[35]

His dual process mode suggests that we can bring rational considerations into balance with the system one gut reactions to which we are so prone. His hope is admirable and comes from a recognition that at a time when technology has given us the capacity to commit acts of horror or kindness across huge distances, the moral equipment that enabled us to handle smaller groups are not always well suited to handling the new kinds of dilemmas that we now face.

In a similar vein, psychologist Paul Bloom discusses these issues in the prologue of his book *Against Empathy*:[36]

I agree that empathy can sometimes motivate kind behavior. But ... it is biased, pushing us in the direction of parochialism and racism. It is short-sighted, motivating actions that might make things better in the short term but lead to tragic results in the future. It is innumerate, favouring the one over the many. It can spark violence, our empathy for those close to us is a powerful force for war and atrocity toward others. It is corrosive of personal relationships; it exhausts the spirit and can diminish the force of kindness and love.

It is an important point. We may laud empathy but need to recognize its limitations too. Bloom points out for example how empathy can be a barrier to good parenting because it makes it hard for us to endure the suffering of our children, which of course we need to be able to do on occasion.

A tendency toward empathy can play havoc with our ability to judge fairly or even to act morally. Empathy-led choices can, for example, limit us through insensitivity to number; which means we can become morally full, replete with charity, if we help just one or two people. Our appetite to help the larger numbers of people whose pain we cannot feel, because they don't provide the individual stories for our empathy to latch on to, is diminished.

If Greene and Bloom are right that we've developed the machinery to work our way to solving competing needs between me and us, but are not so good when it comes to us versus them, what does this say about how we should judge each other's judgements? Do we only applaud the instrumental, system two approach? Should we always admire the tougher parent who can handle their children's pain with equanimity? Neither Bloom nor Greene are saying we should be heartless in that way, but they clearly believe that the reflective system two mode is the better path to good moral judgements. And they clearly have a certain logic on their side.

There is, however, a significant limit to that logic. For what does it say about the right way to judge if only a psychopath would be untroubled by Hawkeye's dilemma. To judge on a utilitarian basis only is to become less than human in a particular sense. To look to being purely rational is something of a dead end in human eyes. We don't like heartless people. We need to know that people care deep down, even as we assess the appropriateness of this caring. For all the merits of being dispassionate, we cannot take seriously someone's capacity to judge without the right kind of emotion in play. The philosophers John Doris and Stephen Stitch put it, echoing Bernard Williams, as follows:

> An ethical conception that commends relationships, commitments, or life projects that are at odds with the sorts of attachments that can reasonably be expected to take root in and vivify actual human lives is an ethical conception with – at best – a very tenuous claim to our assent.[37]

Notwithstanding Bloom's point about the limits of empathy, without the right kind of emotion there is literally no point. We won't ever celebrate the philanthropic psychopath (pursuing fame and adulation) over the loving parent who reads to their child every night. The narrowly utilitarian calculus tells us the psychopath does more good than the individual parent, but this won't stand up in human terms.[38] To be fully human we need

room for this technically irrational but moving response to the
sound of an owl by Rupert Brooke:

The Owl

Downhill I came, hungry, and yet not starved;
Cold, yet had heat within me that was proof
Against the North wind; tired, yet so that rest
Had seemed the sweetest thing under a roof.

Then at the inn I had food, fire, and rest,
Knowing how hungry, cold, and tired was I.
All of the night was quite barred out except
An owl's cry, a most melancholy cry

Shaken out long and clear upon the hill,
No merry note, nor cause of merriment,
But one telling me plain what I escaped
And others could not, that night, as in I went.

And salted was my food, and my repose,
Salted and sobered, too, by the bird's voice
Speaking for all who lay under the stars,
Soldiers and poor, unable to rejoice.

We need to know we have the right emotional tone alongside
how we assess the benefits or costs of an action. Brooke is not
doing anything useful, but his empathy enables us to judge him
well in any case. And not only is this something we must content
ourselves with, the sentimental and emotional responses are also
the source of our meaning and goals. We have preferences and so

judgement will be coloured and shaped by emotion if it is to look recognizably human. Perhaps unfairly sometimes, but without these tinges the world becomes colourless and odourless. So machine-like narrowly utilitarian thinking cannot be where we hope to end up, even if we realize we must not wallow in sentiment.

In any case, even where Greene and Bloom are right to point out that system two rational thinking needs to override the thoughtless urges of system one, this is intrinsically difficult for us because of how we've evolved. After all, what was more important for our ancestors' survival: truth or reputation?[39] Well, it's the latter according to Haidt, who argues that early social humans improved their survival chances not so much by having accurate perceptions of the world, but rather through ensuring they were seen in a positive light by those with whom they needed to cooperate. This means we subordinate 'exploratory thought', which is concerned with trying to get things right, to 'confirmatory thought', which is about looking for evidence that supports our preferences.

Much as we might look to use system two thinking and override the bias prone system one tendency, there's a problem. The processes in question are unconscious and so we don't have access to them frequently enough to alter them. And because they are unconscious, we aren't typically aware of the kind of feedback we would need to learn and change. So we should not assume we can override these reflexes. And experts who think they can use their expertise to battle the tendencies are even worse off. They tend to overestimate their ability to be objective and so are in some ways more prone to those limitations. As Daniel Kahneman himself put it, in fairly provocative form, 'teaching psychology is mostly a waste of time'.

The sobering thought here is that system two–like moral reasoning, when we use it at all, is deployed for tactical reasons in the light of persuading others rather than rational, dispassionate assessment, and recruited to back up those taste-based moral judgements rather than to test them. Instead, its main role is to act as our inner lawyer (in Haidt's words) which is looking for evidence to make a case that justifies our intuitive judgement and, in particular, a case that will hold up in the eyes of others who are critically judging your own judgement. It seems then that even when we are in our more rational moral reasoning mode, this is a version of special pleading and is riven with self-serving motives and post hoc rationalizations. Why do we have this weird mental architecture? As hominid brains tripled in size over the last five million years, developing language and a vastly improved ability to reason, why did we evolve an inner lawyer, rather than an inner judge or scientist? Wouldn't it have been most adaptive for our ancestors to go figure out the truth?[40] The answer is that we evolved to care more about our reputations, and this means it will always be difficult to change someone's view of others (including your own) by appealing to logic or evidence.

The psychologist Philip Tetlock has looked closely at how experts and lay people make judgements and predictions, and has concluded that indeed *confirmatory* thought nearly always trumps *exploratory* thought. Confirmatory thought, as we've seen, is the satisfying tendency to latch upon evidence that confirms your assumptions, as against exploratory thought, which pursues the truth – however inconvenient it may be for your preferences. For Tetlock, exploratory thought only beats confirmatory thought under three conditions:

1 you realize you are accountable to an audience before making the decision;
2 the audience's views are unknown; and
3 you believe the audience is well informed and interested in accuracy.

This is what the edifice of science seeks to achieve (and occasionally does achieve) despite the limitations of each individual scientist. Short of these conditions, 'a central function of thought is making sure one acts in ways that can be persuasively justified or excused to others'.[41] Our job is to persuade, others and ourselves.

We don't have to accept the full evolutionary account for why these features of our moral judgement have arisen to accept the power of the analysis. The word of warning to take away is that when you or I feel certain of our judgements, we should be conscious of the fact that we have many internal mechanisms for creating certainty in our self-serving moral views. Unreliable judgments run through us like a stick of rock. We have prejudices and reputations to protect, alliances to forge.

These insights seem to vindicate a view of human nature set out by David Hume who, as a thoroughgoing naturalist, had prescient insights that have been out of fashion until recently. In contrast with philosophers such as Bentham, Kant and Plato, for whom moral judgement was a rational project – where abstract reasons were themselves sources of moral motivation, Hume said this:

> Morality is nothing in the abstract nature of things, but is entirely relative to the sentiment or mental taste of each particular being, in the same manner as the distinctions of sweet and bitter, hot and cold arise from the particular feeling of each sense or organ. Moral perceptions, therefore, ought not to be classed with the operations of the understanding, but with the tastes or sentiments.[42]

Though it is hard for us to see this and even harder to acknowledge it in ourselves, the evidence from moral psychology seems to bear him out. Haidt describes our conscious self as like the rider on the back of a huge elephant, with the lack of conscious control that image suggests. The reason traditional moral theories don't always resonate with human experience is that they appeal overly to the conscious rider and ignore the fact that the elephant is doing the emotional heavy lifting.[43]

Reserving (or revisiting) judgement

When we enter a new situation in life and are confronted by a new person, we bring with us the prejudices of the past and our previous experiences of people. These prejudices we project upon the new person. Indeed, getting to know a person is largely a matter of withdrawing projections; of dispelling the smoke screen of what we imagine he is like and replacing it with the reality of what he is actually like.

(ANTHONY STORR, QUOTED IN BRYAN MAGEE, *POPPER*
(LONDON, 1973))

In this quotation we see the challenge and the false hope of a solution. Our prejudices, projections and smokescreens, as are our moralizings, self-serving motives and susceptibilities, are numerous and varied as I've discussed in this chapter. The hope that Anthony Storr offers is that without these illusions we can learn to see clearly. This is inspiring advice but ultimately utopian. There is no neutral ground and that's why no one will truly understand you. We are always prone to these tendencies and so it's important to know how to question our judgement rather than deny it exists or wish it away. We might think, with Nick Carraway in *The Great Gatsby*, that 'reserving judgement is a matter of infinite hope', and we might rightly try to suspend judgement so as to give people room to breathe, to develop, to become, rather than boxing them in with hot flashes of assessment – but judging seems to be something we are stuck with, even when we don't notice we are doing it, in part *because* we don't notice.

And even advice that advocates thinking about the beam in your own eye before going for the speck in another's is easier said than done. The reason is that the best liars have convinced themselves and therefore have no need to feel the awkwardness of mixed motives. As Robert Wright puts it in *The Moral Animal*, 'human beings are a species splendid in their array of moral equipment, tragic in their propensity to misuse it, and pathetic in their constitutional ignorance of that misuse'.[44]

As I hope to have shown in this chapter, moralism, inconsistency, self-righteousness, selective loyalty and hypocrisy are our daily bread and these will not be simply overridden when it comes to judging.

That said, there is much to be said for our patterns and styles of judgement for all their flaws. Let's not ignore the tremendous power that comes from these very same moral intuitions. Experimenters may cleverly show the limits of our capacity, rather like those students of human perception who conjure up well known optical illusions to show the limits of our visual system, but we should recognize, as Joshua Greene is keen to point out, how powerful and useful the automatic setting on our dual process camera is most of the time too.

Before we start judging our judgements too harshly, let's remember how well we can behave and cooperate thanks to this capacity to navigate the social world. The news agenda is based on exceptions to the norm: 'if it bleeds, it leads', or alternatively, as one journalist observed, 'dog bites man is not news, while man bites dog certainly is'. Because of this tendency to latch on to the vividly bad, we don't give the boringly good its due. Most of the time people are not biting dogs, most of the time we are just getting along. The lesser told story is that human beings cooperate much of the time. The moral intuitions we have inherited are designed to enable such cooperation on a scale not seen elsewhere in nature. I'm writing this while waiting for a delayed flight, and while I'm frustrated as are others, we've found ways to manage a situation despite all being primarily focused on our own needs, and assessing the world through that lens. We coordinate well enough much of the time.

Whether we denigrate or see strengths in human judgement, there is no way of being without judging. So much of it is happening outside of our awareness, for one thing. And so a true withholding of judgement, in the spirit of Nick Carraway, is as illusory as judging objectively. It is important we recognize this. Rhetorically, the illusion of withholding judgement may even provide a self-serving rationalization of its own: 'I'm not judging you' standing as a withholding of accountability, like 'I'm just teasing' finds a way to get the point across without acknowledgement of the source. What I mean is, if you aren't clear about your judgement of me, then I have no way to challenge or rebut any misconstruals you may have hidden as they are behind another smokescreen, this time of neutrality.

So, what can we do? My own view is since we always judge, let's know we are doing it, know that it is partial at best and revise that judgement in a constant process as we learn more about the person or situation in question. That is to say, recognize your view of someone, but don't settle for it. Find a way to be open to new evidence. One way, following Haidt's advice, is to:

> think of a recent interpersonal conflict with someone you care about and then find one way in which your behaviour was not

exemplary. Maybe you did something insensitive (even if you had a right to do it), or hurtful (even if you meant well) or inconsistent with your principles (even though you can readily justify it). When you first catch sight of a fault in yourself, you'll likely hear frantic arguments from your inner lawyer excusing you and blaming others, but try not to listen. You are on a mission to find at least one thing that you did wrong.

He sees this process, in the spirit of logs and beams, as akin to pulling out a splinter. 'It hurts at first but brings relief, in particular it brings along with it something else, the feeling of honour. And this brings with it a softening of those over-moralized feeling of anger and criticism.'[45]

Another way to revisit judgement, is to see the value in judging while recognizing that whichever view you come to is always open to revision. Imagine a very difficult decision you need to take at some point in the future. Think choosing a school for your child, whether to accept a job that requires you to move to a different city, or whether to move in with someone. It is worth having a provisional view along the way, rather than pretending to be agnostic, even though evidence and argument could sway you from that view to another until such time as the decision has to be taken.

When it comes to judging another person, the decision is never finally taken. There is so much more to know, and so much more than we can ever know. Isn't this why Joseph Conrad reputedly once said 'I have never met a boring man'? The trouble is, we get comfortable with a working theory and lose the imaginative impulse of the literary novelist who is constantly looking at and thinking about their characters and constantly interested in how they make themselves up. And, paradoxically, by constantly judging and revising that judgement, the judgements themselves become less significant for being ubiquitous and they become more contingent because the habits of an ever-changing mind make you less reliant on a singular and inevitably distorted view. This it seems to me is how we can sneak up on revising judgement if not quite reserving it, rather than wishing it away or relying on it too heavily. But the judgement itself is always there, which is why we, at times, dream of escape.

4

Breaking free

I listen with attention to the judgment of all men;
but so far as I can remember,
I have followed none but my own.
(MICHEL DE MONTAIGNE)

During my early years in Baghdad our family would regularly go to the Alwiyah club; a complex of outdoor swimming pool, restaurants, tennis courts and a feeling of perpetual sunshine. If my happiest memories of Iraq can be located anywhere it was there. A highlight in the evenings was the outdoor cinema, which was put together very simply with a large white screen, a projector and fold-up chairs on the grass. Those evenings were intensely exciting for me as a wide-eyed five-year-old. My favourite film was the Disney cartoon *The Jungle Book*, which played frequently on those warm nights. I loved the adventures, the characters, the drama and the songs and the sheer sense of freedom that Mowgli seemed to find in the jungle.[1] I also fantasized that part of my five-year-old self was able to live like

Mowgli, uncluttered by other people, untamed. To escape the constraints of adults and their rules, at least for a while. This film version is just one of many adaptations of Kipling's original stories in his books *The Jungle Book* and *The Second Jungle Book* in which a feral child, starting out wild and unruly, learns over time to assume the burdens of duty and responsibility. Kipling indulged Mowgli's playfulness but he had a moral in tow, and emphasized that these were stories for adults who would need ultimately to learn the reticence and endurance required to manage their too strong, early imaginations. While Kipling would explore the unruly jungle world of Mowgli's early years, there would come a time to put away childish things. This is why his friend Robert Baden-Powell decided to use *The Jungle Book* as a motivational story for his Boy Scout movement. In his original handbook of 1917, junior members became known as wolf cubs, led by the wisdom of Akela – Mowgli's wolf father – and still in use today as the name for Scout leaders.

Watching that film on those nights at the Alwiya club, I was entranced by that strong imagination, but with little use for the stoical restraint that was its required counterpart. I had a streak of recklessness at that time which culminated in many visits to the hospital for stiches and to fix the occasional broken bone. I felt free. And there is part of me that still feels that way. I still need to feel able to shrug off convention and rules and expectations that box me in. I still imagine what it would be like to be able to fly unaided, or to live without judgement.

When I look at how our children are often raised today, bubble-wrapped in overheated, over-protective, over-scheduled safe spaces, I wish for them the more unsupervised unstructured time we used to call 'mucking about'. Unwatched. Beyond that, I feel we should celebrate their essential otherness. Rather than focus on similarities with their parents or each other, it is as well to remember that children are to some extent strange creatures in our midst and, especially when very young, deeply subversive of social norms. How odd the world of adult convention must look to them. When William James commented that a baby's early impressions of the world are a 'great blooming, buzzing confusion', he offered a starting point in describing how a child's view on the world is a long way from how you and I see things. For years they stand outside our concepts of time, norms, control and preoccupations. Before they can worry about being judged, they need to develop an insight into other minds which does not really occur until after a few years of development. The strange animal-like freedom of the young child is something that cannot be maintained through the rigours of growing up; adolescence, for example, being a time of particularly acute concern for the judgement of others. My daughter Anna comments on the intersecting networks of groups at her school, both cliquey and hierarchical, with an everyday tone which belies the daily worry of when to feel accepted, and when rejected.

The name 'Mowgli' was made up by Kipling to mean 'toad' 'in the language of the forest', conveying his nakedness in contrast with his furred friends. When I look back I realize Mowgli offered me a view of life where the ultra-social animal could shed the claustrophobic layers of social norms, and relish a more feral, animal identity. And I doubt I was the only one who felt this way. Partly because of such dreams of escape we can feel an ancient echo of that need for freedom as adults with an abiding taste for being unruly and hoping to be somewhat free of convention, compromise and the judgement of others. A friend commented to me recently how at an intimidatingly formal dinner with starchy linen, an even more starchy waiting staff and a bewildering array of cutlery arrayed on the table, he felt a strong urge to pick up his soup bowl with both hands, put it to his mouth and just *glug*. Intrigued by what is the pure essence of an unsocialized, true self, we are perhaps drawn to the idea of an animal nature, a (not necessarily noble) savage self that stands apart from the dizzying and deafening sounds of human traffic.

Myths and fables of the wolf-boy genre abound, from the legend of Romulus and Remus (who were abandoned by the River Tiber as babies to be found and raised by a wolf) to Tarzan. Alongside these intriguing tales, we occasionally encounter real-life equivalents, true stories of children thrown free of civilization, which equally draw our attention and curiosity. Francois Truffaut's film *The Wild Child* and Werner Herzog's *The Enigma of Kaspar Hauser* are both cinematic treatments of such real-life cases.

Even if what King Lear called 'the thing itself' is a diminished form of life, even if 'unaccommodated man is no more but such a poor, bare, forked animal ...',[2] we relish the chance to see our atavistic, uncivilized selves develop outside the never-ending gaze and expectations of other people.[3] This chapter is about this urge to be free of human judgement.

Figure 4.1 *Mowgli, by John Lockwood Kipling (father of Rudyard Kipling). An illustration from* The Second Jungle Book *(1895).*

Animals and artists

In a real-life reversal of the wolf-boy legend, the philosopher Mark Rowlands tells of how he adopted a wolf cub who lived with him every day for the following eleven years. The intensity of the relationship is poignantly described in his memoir *The Philosopher and the Wolf*. Brenin, the wolf, is with Rowlands throughout every part of his day, whether lecturing, cooking or playing rugby. Rowlands clearly had the deepest respect and admiration (as well as love) for his constant companion, and would often find the human world relatively degraded by comparison. In his book he venerates the purity and honesty of his Brenin over the ape-like human, whom he sees as preoccupied by calculations around how to manage, impress, seduce and steal from other people.

> If you want to understand the soul of the wolf – the essence of the wolf, what the wolf is all about – then you should look at the way the wolf moves. And the crabbed and graceless bustling of the ape, I came to realise with sadness and regret, is an expression of the crabbed and graceless soul that lies beneath.[4]

Rowlands's love for the clean honesty of the wolf over the complex mess of intrigue and backstabbing that typifies the ape is an expression of how much better things would be if only humans could be more like wolves. But this is a gap that looks hard to cross. Could there ever be a pre-lapsarian truly wild child? As the Wikipedia entry on the wolf-boy puts it:

Legendary and fictional children are often depicted as growing up with relatively normal human intelligence and skills and an innate sense of culture or civilization, coupled with a healthy dose of survival instincts. Their integration into human society is made to seem relatively easy.

At the end of *The Jungle Book* Mowgli doesn't look anything like a wolf-boy entering into human civilization. He looks more like a very human migrant moving from one culture to another. The gap between humans and all other animals is much debated and there is a long list of candidate suggestions about what marks people off, including language, planning and foresight, ability to use tools, cultural evolution and many, many more. But the key difference that is most relevant to this book is to do with how we are hyper-invested in coalitions. The evolutionary psychologist John Tooby has identified coalitional instincts as a profound break from the rest of the animal kingdom. According to Tooby, the coalitional instinct – the ability to organize into teams – is what enabled groups of less powerful individuals to compete with more dominant alpha males. In teams, two can beat one, three can beat two, etc. … Yet the many benefits of that degree of coordination and cooperation are not something other animals seem to have cottoned on to in the same degree that humans have. As a consequence, we are profoundly shaped by the groups of which we can claim to be members.

You are a member of a coalition only if someone (such as you) interprets you as being one, and you are not if no one does. We project coalitions onto everything, even where they have no place, such as in science. We are identity-crazed.[5]

In order to make its way in the world, any creature of a certain complexity needs to make relatively successful judgements. Unless the creature is able to perceive and assess its environment it can hardly get by. Predator and prey can only function effectively with finely sensitized judgements of threat versus safety, or even the distance to be covered in the final attack. But not only do all animals judge the objects and physical spaces that surround them, they also judge each other in a ceaseless round of second-guessing. Unlike when judging which branches will hold while attempting to climb a tree, a cat chasing a mouse must anticipate what its prey might be thinking. And the mouse, second-guessing in turn, might change its course based on guessing what the cat has been guessing. This tit-for-tat complexity is built into the social encounters of most sentient beings.

Move into the human world and you see things get dramatically more complicated. We ultra-social language-using animals have taken the extra step of benefiting from cooperation and competition within and across groups. This has provided enormous gains that result from a higher level of human coordination but has also created the conditions in which cheats and free-riders can thrive, giving us far more options to persuade and mislead. So now our guesswork requires second- and third-guessing and an explosion of overlapping, often unconscious, revisions follows.

We need big brains to manage this arms race of thought and counter-thought. It is a familiar fact that humans are born underdeveloped relative to other mammals. A baby deer or calf will walk and feed itself within hours of birth. A human baby needs to mature for at least ten years after birth to become relatively independent and a further ten years to reach full maturity. Our brains are much bigger than other mammals and need to continue to develop outside the uterus, not only so that the mother can walk upright and still be able to give birth, but so that the socializing mechanisms the brain needs in order to reach its potential can kick in.

Brain sizes vary by mammal population, with humans being the largest. Of all the things that might correlate with brain size, the best correlation across the animal kingdom is that of the social groups they inhabit. While chimpanzees live in groups of around thirty and maintain those bonding relationships through enormous amounts of grooming, humans can work in groups upwards of 150 and still maintain that sense of belonging and recognition of each other. The anthropologist Robin Dunbar has suggested that language evolved to take the place of grooming and thereby massively extended the number of people who can form true stable bonds,[6] and to handle 150 people we need something like action at a distance. The peculiarly human mechanism that he offers, which enables reputations to rise and fall over distances that grooming could never manage, is gossip. Someone once quipped that a secret is a thing you tell just one other person. Put that habit of loose talk out across a population and you see the development of a policing mechanism that paradoxically can create the foundation of trust and social cooperation. Reputations thereby change through hearsay and word of mouth.

We are unusual animals. In the last chapter, I discussed how our naïve realism leans us toward a self-image as individual, atomistic rational agents experiencing life as though peering out on the world through a window. And like the fish that swims unaware of the water in which it is suspended, we struggle to see the social reality in which our actions are meaningfully conducted. And if we miss the social reality in which we operate, we also ignore the vast iceberg of unconscious work that sits below the tip of conscious thought. A century of work in psychology has borne out Freud's insight that our egos are not masters in their own house. As we saw in the last chapter, explorations in implicit bias, cognitive illusions and the insights of moral psychology repeatedly show we don't have a clear grasp on our reasons for doing and thinking the things that we do. Over the centuries, going back to Plato, many have debated the relationship between reason and emotion and how these are tangled through the texture of human judgement. On the one hand, you have those who declare that reason drives judgement first and foremost; on the other, thinkers like David Hume who declare that 'reason is and must always be the slave of the passions'.

The evidence laid out in the last chapter shows that Hume got it right. When it comes to how we judge each other, especially around what is right and wrong, we start with emotion-led intuitions and only retrospectively furnish them with logical-sounding reasons. In their book *The Enigma of Reason*, Hugo Mercier and Dan Sperber point out that reason is essentially deployed argumentatively. We are prone to the various biases and heuristics discussed in the last chapter because our aim is not to make logical inferences, rather it is to be so persuasive.

Jonathan Haidt puts it well: 'the world we live in is not really made of rocks, trees and physical objects; it is a world of insults, opportunities, status symbols, betrayals, saints and sinners'.[7] Unlike the wolf, we need to travel through this world with an understanding that our prospects for flourishing depend heavily on how skilfully we judge others and how well we are judged in return. While judgement is often partial and skewed, we don't all deploy it with the same skill. Some people are better at noticing, more perceptive, more interested and thus able adduce more evidence in making assessments of others, than those who are self-absorbed and incurious. That said, there is no way to fully avoid the limitations of judgement, given the constraints of time and attention and the impossibility of knowing the full story (as we will explore further in the next chapter).

We may want to escape the world of judgement, but we are stuck with it, and stuck with doing it in a peculiar way, riven as we are with conflicting motives and partial perceptions. The selves we inhabit are so deeply constituted by society, and a human network of meanings, that a wolf-boy is an oxymoron and makes little sense in reality. The anthropologist Clifford Geertz once described culture as a set of 'control mechanisms – plans, recipes, rules, instructions – for the governing of behavior'.[8] Put like that we can see all the more why we might fantasize about throwing off those shackles. But, for Geertz, while almost all other animals have their own control mechanisms wired in by biology humans 'desperately depend' on cultural programs learned, like Mowgli did, and can only 'complete themselves' in particular social settings. Freed from culture, Geertz concludes humans would not be free as a bird, they would be 'unworkable monstrosities with very few useful instincts, fewer recognisable sentiments, and no intellect: mental basket cases'. The gulf between the human and the animal world is in this respect pretty unbridgeable. Wittgenstein, looking at it the other way around, observed that 'If a lion could speak, we could not understand him.'[9]

And what is true of our forms of life in general is equally true when you focus on the challenge to be free of artifice at any one moment. We often talk of people as being independently minded, authentic, irreverent, original but we always do so in a way that is shadowed by the cultural context in which they are speaking or acting. Take for instance the novelist Stendahl's doomed obsession with the idea of 'becoming natural'. He decided to 'say whatever comes into my head, to say it simply and without pretension; to avoid striving for an effect in conversation'.[10] He decided that he would only succeed if 'I learn to show my indifference'. And here we can see some of the tension in the ideal. *Learning* to be *indifferent*, like trying to look relaxed, is a case of 'willing what cannot be willed'. Even to express the idea of 'authenticity' is to do so in words of others' making.

We can never then be meaningfully free of social influence. But the fantasy of the wolf-boy persists nevertheless. He speaks to a deep desire to be free that animates us to varying degrees, however hopeless, both in terms of the desire to be free from the gaze of others, but also (for those lucky enough to feel strong) to be free to invent themselves, to shape and to overcome. To be socially constituted is to be clothed, and yet dreams of shedding that confining raiment are valuable in many ways. An undertow of rebellion that will not bow down to the expectations of others is a powerful and creative urge, however persistent the judgements that pulse through our everyday encounters. The urge to break rules, to undermine power, to assert a distinctive and individual voice produces some of the richest and most deeply satisfying experiences in our lives.

W.B. Yeats's poem 'A Coat' advocates shaking off those fetters:

I MADE my song a coat
Covered with embroideries
Out of old mythologies
From heel to throat;
But the fools caught it,
Wore it in the world's eyes
As though they'd wrought it.
Song, let them take it,
For there's more enterprise
In walking naked.

While it makes no sense to try to be as free and natural as a wolf, creators of art like Yeats have demonstrated other ways to break free, if only against a backdrop of human culture. He was, after all, the same poet asking his loved one to 'Tread softly because you tread on my dreams'. The artistic impulse to freedom is often framed as the abandonment of the judgement of others. We see countless examples of artists as less encumbered than most – more eccentric, more original, more troubled. The literary critic Harold Bloom describes the 'strong poet' as one not overshadowed by the 'anxiety of influence' and whose originality, such as it is, comes from the need to shrug off those antecedents. He uses the term 'misprision' to describe how strong poets misread or misinterpret their literary predecessors in order to create a fresh imaginative space for themselves to occupy. Those unencumbered artists aspire to a kind of truthfulness (by abandoning convention) while sacrificing everyday accountability to The Truth in a stricter sense. Oscar Wilde, in his 1892 essay 'The Decay of Lying', celebrated the fact that 'Lying, the telling of beautiful untrue things, is the proper aim of Art' and warned us against the dangers of 'lapsing into mere accuracy'.

But this rebellious spirit is not just for artists and poets. Since Freud 'democratized genius', by revealing that we each have an unruly and creative unconscious shadowing our rational selves, we have come to see it is for us all to drink on occasion from a subversive well of complexity.[11] Thanks to Freud our self-image has been expanded to accommodate the irrational, the unruly, the unacceptable and the turbulent. We each have ways of expressing the private thought that we are unlike the image other people have of us. We have self-destructive urges, strange fantasies, particular anxieties and obsessions. The psychoanalyst D.W. Winnicott venerates something of the uncivilized and unruly in us all by offering that 'we are poor indeed if we are only sane'.

And there are less dramatic ways to establish independence of the judgement of others. Therapeutic advice suggests we seize days, take paths less travelled, release the power within and so on. These over-magnifications of common sense venerate the power of positive thinking and resilience to get us out of the bind of self-doubt and self-blame as though this can be done in an act of sheer will. Everyday tactics to quiet the chatter involve common distractions such as channel surfing, alcohol, drugs and sex. Some people achieve the same through meditation, and approaches drawing on Eastern or Stoic philosophy, which encourage fostering ego-scepticism (realizing that you are egocentric, that you do not have an accurate view of the world and that most people aren't really thinking about you after all). We find ways to recognize the harm in pursuing judgement, making us cramped, needy and manipulative, and the deep satisfaction that comes from imagining we can break free.

Escaping the potent audience

One of the reasons the judgement of others can be so wearing is to do with how hard it is to control *which* audiences matter *most*. Haven't we all had the feeling that we really shouldn't be bothered by a particular person's opinion of us? They are too ignorant, irrelevant, unkind to be a valid judge of the 'true' you. And yet their opinion sticks in your craw anyway? I can still remember the maths teacher in primary school who falsely accused me of trying to cheat on the test back in 1976, though I'm sure he hasn't thought of that event since. This power certain others have over us is hard to explain and difficult to escape. And frustratingly, efforts to dim the potency of audiences tend to be self-defeating. Whether trying to diminish the memory of an admonishing father, or the opinion of an annoying colleague, we only reveal our helplessness to ourselves.

A new romantic infatuation can play havoc with self-respect. Interests, duties, friendships are put on hold as we give way to the unpredictable gaze of the significant other. Even while the rational brain looks on wincing at our antics, we re-work normality in so many ways to court good opinion. Every time a friend of mine would show a sudden new interest in geology, folk music or modernist literature, I'd know there was a new woman in his life. The new love is always a very potent audience, and we only really care about the judgement of potent others.

Similarly, it is frustrating to see how little we care about the good opinion of those who have no potency for us. When we consider counting the blessings supplied by well-meaning friends, it is hard to give these the weight they might deserve. You *expect* good news from a fan and discount it accordingly. Often people who are 'on your side' can do little to boost your self-esteem, however many plaudits and compliments they offer. In fact, it is precisely because you are not hazarding the risk of social pain when faced with their judgement that you cannot take pleasure from such good news. An audience of adoring fans becomes more impotent the more you can take it for granted because judgement only has weight if we risk being judged ill. And we respond to ill judgement by giving it more weight because we don't imagine it has been conjured up for effect. It is therefore likely to be the source of more genuine information, however uncomfortable to hear and thus making the provider of the critique somewhat more potent.[12] This may explain the peculiar prevalence of advice on 'negging', faint praise mingled with critique designed to destabilize someone, as a way to chat people up.

The pursuit of freedom described in this chapter is often to do with driving off the nagging dependency we have on audiences we cannot control. The harder thing to acknowledge is that the deeper motive is often to win the best applause of all, that which comes from showing we do not need it. So, freedom and judgement are in this sense inextricably linked.

In *Houdini's Box* Adam Phillips explores the vagaries of the pursuit of freedom by looking at the life of the ultimate escapologist Harry Houdini. The box that encases him is crucial to the illusion of freedom. In the old philosophical distinction between freedom *to* express and pursue and freedom *from* imposition and constraints, much of our vulnerable hope to escape is expressed as freedom from, at least for the majority who feel they do not have much power most of the time. Thus Houdini voluntarily incarcerates himself so as to break free. This way he holds his audience. Aside from the physical challenge itself Houdini needs to manage his audience further. His reputation is self-made so he gives poignant reassurances that he has worked hard (is honest and fair) and that he studies, etc. 'Houdini knows that what he is always working on, what he has to work with, is his audience's scepticism. Without scholarship, without any kind of institutional position, unentitled, Houdini is in the business of persuasion.' And so are we all. It turns out the desire to be free is often just another way of trying to court the right kind of applause, a theme that shadows our lives from the moment we learn we are immersed in a culture that is larger than us and whose ways we must learn, and on some level reject, in order to be truly accepted. We are nothing without an audience, nothing without their judgements. And this doomed struggle for freedom is central to being judged well; if Houdini were simply free, then no one would bother to watch.

The need to manage audiences comes with a deeper set of mixed feelings we have toward them. On the one hand we need them and on the other we resent the power they can have over us. We make choices at different stages of our lives or within daily encounters that show us up as riven by ambivalence toward other people. Facing them one minute and turning our backs the next. A willingness to overcome the need to play to the audience, a determination to be self-reliant, authentic, unconventional, ironic or experimental can lead to wonderful acts of creativity, invention and heroism. And, of course, as these creative projects succeed, like a successful metaphor drifting into cliché, they become the new norms that future generations will need to subvert.

In my book *The Happiness Paradox* I explored how this need to be free has a paradoxical relationship with the need to be justified in the eyes of potent others. If you try too hard to be judged well, to control your audience, you are likely to fail, because the audience has been tamed to the point of impotence where their judgement no longer matters. Like the comedian bowing to canned laughter there is something intrinsically unsatisfying about organizing your own applause. And you risk coming across as craven and needy by looking like you're trying too hard to please. No, instead the only path to feeling justified involves travelling in the opposite direction. Toward the rebellious desire to escape from judges and forge your own path irrespective of who might be looking and what they might think. Only by developing personal projects that don't look around the sides for approval makes you worthy of achieving justification. But here the paradox becomes more obvious, because if you are to pursue freedom too successfully you will have left the audience behind and become incoherent or unacceptable, so you need to turn back to face them again. The move between these two needs is subtle and complex. It is so easy to see the contrast in binary terms – now I'm free and now I'm judged – but that isn't how these themes play out in life at all. They work off and through each other in ways that are hard to disentangle. This interaction is so fluid and nuanced that it seems informative to turn to literature to bring out the strange interplay more vividly.

Washing off the human stain

Philip Roth's *The Human Stain* dramatizes in remarkable detail the hard work of trying to be justified and the fantasy of escaping those judgements. The protagonist is Coleman Silk, a classics professor at Athena, a (fictional) small liberal arts college in New England. Having achieved a highly respected academic and administrative career, Coleman is caught in a row which gets out of hand. While commenting about two of his students who never turn up to class, Coleman refers to them as 'spooks'. They happen to be black (his bad luck since he had never laid eyes on them) and this leads to accusations of racism and ultimately to a disgraced end to his career. Throughout the imbroglio, Coleman is adamant he did not intend that meaning of the word, but only meant to describe these absent students as ghostly spirits. He loses the argument and loses his job, and is left bitter and humiliated.

From this opening Roth takes us back into Coleman's pre-history and forward into his future via the narrator Nathan Zuckerman.[13] In the story we see Coleman repeatedly try and fail to escape the judgement of others, 'to take the future into his own hands rather than to leave it to an unenlightened society to determine his fate', and learn something about a very human ambivalence toward other people, how we need to turn our backs on the judging crowd while taking the risk at times of becoming intimate with a select few. This is risky because it opens us up to the pain that our escapism has sought, all along, to avoid. The relationships Coleman has with his family, with lovers, with colleagues and with Nathan, his only male friend, tell us much about betrayal, hurt, intimacy, connection and hope. In exploring Coleman's particular story, many of the general themes of this book will hopefully become more tangible, specifically the frailty of mutual knowledge and the complexities of social and moral judgement even as we hope to escape it.

Coleman as a classics professor is well versed in the Greek tragedies which tell of our fateful destinies, but all the while he rages against this sense of inevitability in his own life and against conformity. He decides early on in life that he does not have to live like a tragic character, that he can make choices that push against the grand plans others may have for him. 'This has been

the purpose of the mighty gods. Silky's freedom. The raw I. All the
subtlety of being silky silk.' And when his escape routes prove at
times to be dead ends we see him trapped in the uncomprehending
web of misconstruals and misunderstandings of others. The
subtlety, the 'raw I', of being Coleman is only glimpsed by us,
through the words of Nathan, his narrator. Coleman speaks to
the part of us with an urge to escape the swim of human culture
and the feeling of being trapped by destiny and acquiescence. This
starts out as a form of negative liberty, the urge to be free *from* the
uncomprehending gaze of others. For Coleman, however, there
is a particular motivation. We learn how throughout his life he
has been carrying an, in retrospect, deeply ironic secret. He is in
fact a light-skinned black man (light enough to hide his identity
from nearly everyone) who has had to reject his family and risk
everything to reinvent himself as white. This extraordinary project
of will and deception to deny his origins and ethnicity comes
with many sacrifices along the way, starting with his family. The
overlapping themes of judgement of self and by others along with
attempts to break free could hardly be better illustrated.[14]

It is difficult to say exactly when Coleman decides to foreclose
on his black identity and pass for white. One turning point is
the death of his immensely authoritative father. It was a pivotal
moment for Coleman to lose such an uncompromising figure of
great integrity and as potent an audience as he was an understated
man. When he dies, Coleman finds that:

... to be no longer circumscribed and defined by his father
was like finding that all the clocks wherever one looked

> had stopped and all the watches, and there was no way of knowing what time it was. ... It was, like it or not, his father who had been making up Coleman's story for him; now he would have to make it up for himself and the prospect was terrifying ... (107)

And then it wasn't. Suddenly, the fear of freedom turns into a huge sense of power and self-command for Coleman. He unshackles himself from his potent audience and therefore feels giddily free from that forbidding gaze; at the same time there is also a more positive version of freedom kindled in him. I don't mean positive in a moral sense, rather the active form of freedom, known as freedom *to* (rather than *from*). This form of freedom is as amoral as it is powerful and can lead in unpredictable directions. His father (like his elder brother) had been a voice of conscience for many years and now there is a vacuum to fill.

> With both bulwarks gone – the big brother overseas and the father dead – he is repowered and free to be whatever he wants, free to pursue the hugest aim, the confidence right in his bones to be the particular I. Free on a scale unimaginable to his father.

The disorientating quality of this amoral freedom is rendered all the more stark by contrasting it with the oppressive constraints that were his father's inevitable lot. But along with the exhilarations that come from such an unshackling, comes a feeling of vertigo.

> As free as his father had been unfree. Free now not only of his father but of all that his father had ever had to endure.

The impositions. The humiliations. The obstructions. The wound and the pain and the posturing and the shame – all the inward agonies of failure and defeat. Free instead on the big stage. Free to go ahead and be stupendous. Free to enact the boundless, self-defining drama of the pronouns we, they and I. (109)

It is for Coleman now to work out how to fill this void. After his father's death Coleman drops out of university and joins the navy: a white man in search of adventure. But this new-found freedom, he discovers, does not come for free. There is a raging, almost desperate, drama in Coleman's new discovered, boundless and self-defining way in the world. Unmoored and unshackled, his decision space is now indefinitely wide. It is hard to find a coherent way to be when you have thrown away your compass, maps and fundamental reference points. The potent witnesses of his early life will not be so easily overcome. One evening he gets into a drunken fight with bouncers in a whites-only brothel who recognize that he is black. The night is filled with physical and psychological wretched pain for Coleman and at some point, too drunk to remember, he marks it indelibly onto his skin by getting a US Navy tattoo. He later decides that this has been the worst night of his life, for while at such a very low ebb, we hear the self-loathing recriminations put in the voice of his late father, an audience so potent for Coleman that he is cowed in his arrogant deceptions by 'the unequivocal legitimacy of an upright man' even long after his death. Coleman in his despair begins to gain an insight into the harm he has caused his loved ones in pursuit of this freedom. In Freudian terms the admonishing father of his super-ego is punishing him for allowing his id to express itself untrammelled.

> Is this where you've come, Coleman, to seek the deeper meaning of existence? A world of love, that's what you had, and instead you forsake it for this! The tragic, reckless thing that you've done! And not just to yourself – to us all … What else grandiose are you planning Coleman Brutus? Whom next are you going to mislead and betray? (183)

Brutus, Coleman Silk's middle name, clues us through classical reference to the nature of disloyalty and the difficulty of escaping one's tragic fate.

Those painful, intrusive, thoughts notwithstanding, Coleman maintains his deception and after his return from the navy develops an intense relationship with a beautiful, blond white woman called Steena Paulsson. Steena thinks that Coleman is white. His fledgling experiments in autonomy are temporarily overwhelmed in a different way as he falls completely in love with her. Nathan Zuckerman explains that she was 'voodoo ish in her power … [and] had achieved a startling supremacy over a will as ruthlessly independent as Coleman's …' (118).

In discovering Steena, Coleman discovers the immensity of lust, love and connection but with an undertow of fear that his secret will be revealed. For Coleman, physicality is crucial to the capacity to be lost in another without judgement. In the mode of the atavistic animal self, uncurbed by culture, he finds sex to be a great enabler of unselfconscious connection with Steena and which temporarily keeps his anxieties at bay. Despite the biblical suggestion that to have sex is to 'know' someone, there is something in this depiction of physicality that is to do with acceptance rather than knowledge. Physical connection in this context does not require recognition; by side-stepping head and heart, it can be just about holding tight. But when they are not enmeshed in this melt of physicality he is constantly fearful of discovery. He finds a poem she wrote about her feelings for him. Her poem terrifies him, as he hunts for hidden indications that she has discovered his secret, including misreading the word 'neck' for 'negro'.

Steena presents a turning point now that Coleman sees how his freedom is compromised by the fear of discovery. If he is to have a chance of a life with her he needs to stop hiding. He decides all he can do is to reveal his true story to her by taking her back to meet his black family. The meeting goes well enough, in its somewhat brittle and awkward but kind-spirited mode. But on the train home she turns to him in tears and says that she 'just can't do it' and runs away. His hope of acceptance is crushed when she discovers his, to him, very literal stain. And despite all his belief in the power of actively choosing a singular life, he is defeated and 'he learned how accidentally a destiny is made ... On the other hand, how accidental fate may seem when things can never turn out other than they do'. The Greek fates turn out to have more power than his mere will (127).

He will not make that mistake again. Having been so badly burned in his attempt at vulnerable transparency, Coleman has learned a lesson that sets him on an unavoidable path of denial and deception. So when he meets and decides to marry

Iris he chooses to create a more permanent identity for himself as a white Jewish man to match the culture and religion of his prospective wife. In order to do this, he must write his family out of his story and say that his parents are dead. To complete the process of eradication he returns to tell his mother of his choice in a passage that is both appalling and poignant. As Coleman is talking she realizes she will never be allowed to see her grandchildren, though he offers that she can sit at the corner of the park while he walks them past her in their Sunday best. She says she will be Mrs Brown, looking on from secret corners, and asks whether this devastating rejection of his family and history is all so his children's hair will blow in the wind?[15]

The chapter is called 'Slipping the Punch'. The language of brutality is deliberately reminiscent of an earlier effort to throw off his history. Coleman was once a talented and skilful boxer, but was forced to reject his identity in another turning point when he smashes down a black man in the ring too quickly and the trainer in the audience says he deprived the crowd of a good drama. The physical violence he showed in the ring was necessary to shrugging off his identity then, and echoes the psychological violence he must do to shrug off his mother. Her response is restrained, dignified and all the more powerful a judgement for that. She concludes: 'I suppose any profound change in life involves saying "I don't know you" to someone' (140).

Despite the importance of his relationship with his mother, Coleman absorbs her quiet but potentially devastating judgement. Her restrained expression of disapproval at her son's extraordinary effort to abandon his history is something he can withstand. 'Only through this test can he be the man he has chosen to be, unalterably separated from what he was handed at birth, free to struggle at being free like any human being would wish to be free' (139).

When we embark on major projects of such wilful self-assertion – think of those who choose to leave their partners and children for a new life – we inevitably reckon with the gaze of our once potent audiences. Either we submit to their judgement by reversing our course or hiding our rebellion, or we overcome their judgement by removing their potency. When his brother Walt discovers what Coleman has decided and what he has done to their mother, he responds much more bluntly but Coleman can also withstand this more overtly harsh judgement. In fact the force of Walt's attack pushes Coleman further away from his family ties. Having crossed over once and for all into a new identity, he leaves his family behind – 'throw the punch, do the damage, and forever lock the door' (139) – Coleman embarks on a new life with Iris, a combative marriage during which he has four very white children. Throughout, his secret is kept resolutely safe.

This pivotal reworking of Coleman's life is a grand act of self-determination, a defining choice so extreme that it suggests there was even more driving him to be capable of such cruelty to his family and such extreme denial of his identity (335). Zuckerman the narrator comments, to tell his mother:

> ... it's over. This love affair is over. You're no longer my mother and never were. Anybody who has the audacity to do that

doesn't just want to be white. He wants to be able to do that. It has to do with more than just being blissfully free. It's like the savagery in *The Iliad*, Coleman's favourite book about the ravening spirit of man ...(335)

It's almost to recognize a sociopathic strand in himself which is more than free, it is powerful enough to break free of moral queasiness. It is to demolish humility and access the Nietzschean Superman within, capable of imposing himself on the world through sheer will. But to what end? In *The Gay Science* Nietzsche draws on a remarkable metaphor to describe the power of alternating between change and renewal which reminds me of Coleman in a way:

How greedily the wave approaches as if it were after something! How it crawls with terrifying haste into the inmost nooks of this labyrinthine cliff! It seems that something of value, of great value, must be hidden there. – And now it comes back, a little more slowly but still quite white with excitement; is it disappointed? Has it found what it looked for? Does it pretend to be disappointed? – But already another wave is approaching, still more greedily and savagely than the first, and its soul, too, seems to be full of secrets and the last to dig up treasures. Thus live waves – thus live we who will – more I shall not say.[16]

Fast-forward again to the latter phase of his life, and we return to Coleman being brought low by the indignity of false accusations at Athena college. After all his twisting and turning during a life of cover-ups, hopes of freedom and costly betrayals along the way, Coleman's life threatens to end with him ignominiously and ironically disgraced as a racist, a fatefully tragic turn of events worthy of the Greek literature Coleman immersed himself in all his life.

This would have been the end for Coleman had it not been for a redemptive relationship with a much younger white woman, an illiterate cleaner at the college called Faunia Farley. At one level this looks like yet another one of Coleman's exploitations in a long line of ruthless self-indulgence. There's a moment when Coleman sees it this way too. He watches Faunia on the grass with the other janitors and suddenly sees himself as a monster. Watching her stretch out on the grass and laughing 'exposed him to the last underside of his own disgrace' (157).

But Faunia is not to be underestimated – she is much stronger than that. And in her way, she is saving him. She is helping him recover that sense of independence and freedom, following the assaults he has faced, but with her at his side. She herself was the product of thirty-four years of 'savage surprises', from child abuse at the hands of her stepfather, to the loss of her two children in a fire; the resulting negative wisdom led to finding her own modes of escape throughout her life. She had attempted suicide twice. But her qualities survive the appalling suffering she has endured. Coleman, as narrated by Nathan, says 'she's not religious, she's not sanctimonious, she is not deformed by the fairy tale of purity, whatever other perversions may have disfigured her. She's not interested in judging – she's seen too much for all that shit' (341). It turns out her illiteracy is in fact a pretence. She can read but prefers to hide this fact. Her menial cleaning work allows her to be hard on herself; to scrub away at her stains despite the impossibility of purity. In an echo of the wolf-boy, she says 'I am a crow' and 'alien to the core'. We now see how her pretended illiteracy was part of her power. 'She has nothing against reading per se – it's that pretending not to be able to feels right to her. It spices things up. She just cannot get enough of the toxins: of all that you're not supposed to be, to show, to say, to think but that you are and show and say and think whether you like it or not' (297).

Coleman takes comfort in his relationship with Faunia despite the scandal in which he has become mired. With her he can aim to live 'beyond their indictment. Beyond their judgement. Learn, he told himself, before you die, to live beyond the jurisdiction of their enraging, loathsome, stupid blame'. He sees how her dignified, unyielding stance toward the world is his way of escaping the judgement of others. He tells himself he will 'take the hammer of Faunia to everything outlived, all the exalted justifications, and smash [his] way to freedom. ... From the ridiculous quest for significance. From the never ending campaign for legitimacy' (171).

It was enough to be able to conduct themselves like two people who had nothing whatsoever in common, all the while remembering how they could distil down to an orgasmic essence everything about them that was irreconcilable, the human discrepancies that produced all the power. (47)

Again, the orgasmic essence is important to Coleman. He believes in the possibility for sex to offer something good for both in its own right. A place free from judgement and blame, he writes in the spirit of Gore Vidal's observation that 'sex is the one purely existential act … Sex builds no roads, writes no novels … gives no meaning to anything in life but itself'. There is something about sex that reveals those animal natures to a self whether a wolf or a crow that has escaped the mess of human traffic. As in his moments of physicality with Steena (sex and a memorable 'slithery dance'), Coleman takes sanctuary in a wordless bond. And before he can look for something more articulated than that, Faunia is clear-eyed in her unsentimental warning to Coleman: 'don't fuck it up pretending it is something else' (203).[17] Despite her hardened carapace of self-protection, Faunia for the first time in her life starts freeing herself to love Coleman. She begins to trust him, and appreciate his own troubles and sees in him a generosity that he never saw in himself. Coleman in turn trusts her enough to tell her his secret; accepting and finding acceptance.

> [Faunia] wanted to know what is the worst. Not the best, the worst. By which she meant the truth. What is the truth? So he told it to her. Because he loved her at that moment, imagining her scrubbing the blood … he loved her. Because that is when you love somebody – when you see them being game in the face of the worst. Not courageous. Not heroic. Just game. (340)

In this light, we can see the connection that has developed between the two as about embracing each other's vulnerability and thus accepting it in themselves. But this is just where it is possible to be hurt in a relationship. As this growing trust and openness develops it stumbles painfully at one point; there is a sharp shift of registers triggered by Coleman when reading out a story from the newspaper to Faunia. He should have known better than to read to her, and Faunia, shamed by the reminder of the intellectual gulf between them, runs from him. Having numbed herself with her crow-like, alien hardness she feels punished for relaxing her guard. She leaves to find Prince, a real crow she has known and loved for many years, now caged in a local Audubon Society. But Prince is caged because he once briefly escaped and was nearly killed by fellow crows as he, having been hand-raised by humans, had the wrong crow voice. This crow had been ruined by the human stain and was no longer fit for the company of wild creatures. Real crows are really free. This one has been caught up in our mire. Faunia punishes herself for trusting anyone, and daring to hope we can ever shrug off the human stain which is 'indwelling. Inherent. Defining'. 'It's why all the cleansing is a joke. A barbaric joke at that' (242).

That was Faunia in her despair, talking in the wrong voice and feeling doomed because of it. All her cleaning will never purify her and will never remove the stigmata of a damaged self. It will never remove the risk of shame. But for Roth the search for purity is a strange Christian overhang, and to be contrasted with Coleman's beloved Greeks. The wolfish or crow-like appearance of stainlessness does not suit the human condition. 'The fantasy of purity is appalling' (242), but Roth is showing that it is widespread and persistent nevertheless.

The pursuit of purity and of washing off human stains is closely linked to the fear of shame explored in Chapter 1. Brené Brown in her popular TedTalk on shame addresses this fear in a way that sheds light on what Coleman and Faunia and all of us at times find ourselves doing. We numb vulnerability, she says. We feel fragile with no guarantees, so we numb the possibility of shame and fear. We use devices such as bingeing and develop addictions but that way we numb joy, gratitude, happiness. We make the uncertain certain, for example with religion, and find ways to perfect ourselves, which can bring a partisan hardening and blame into our judgement of others.

She feels we need to embrace our vulnerability and have courage, with its etymological root *cour* at its heart. To be whole hearted is to allow compassion to oneself as well as to others. To allow weaknesses and vulnerability, by recognizing this is necessary, is the willingness to say 'I love you' first, the willingness to operate without guarantees, and to let ourselves be seen. Children, she notes, are not perfect, they are wired for struggle. And we were all once impure children. And we do not stop struggling.

Faunia through suffering, and Coleman through striving and failing to be free, have learned that and have found each other. Talking of Prince the crow, Faunia 'in a strange voice of her own' said 'I love that strange voice'. And this was also what Coleman loved about Faunia. Real love is possible because it recognizes that others will see past your clean surfaces, will see your stains and decide if they like their flavour, tone and texture. Steena could not do that for Coleman, Iris never saw them and so never

knew him that well, but Faunia could and did. She saw him, and
he saw her and they liked what they saw and accepted what they
still did not know of each other. 'She is not deformed by the fairy
tale of purity whatever other perversions might have disfigured
her' (340).

Fundamentally, the urge to be free is the best way to receive
a satisfying measure of its opposite, and a theme of this book:
the chance to be judged well. For this tentative hope I'd say is
the defining mark of the human condition. Noam Chomsky
once offered that the urge to be free is our essential and defining
property, but I sense the opposite. We are apes not wolves.
Despite our hopes of escape we cannot make sense of ourselves
without approving witnesses, judges who offer significance
through applause, love, approval, acceptance, status, trust among
many other forms of justification. These are the potent audiences
who we might betray or hurt, and who might do the same to us.
There are complex interlocking themes here, but ultimately the
dream our stains might be washed free, however heroic, however
violent, is forlorn, so instead our stains must be accepted, if not
always understood, by others and thanks to them, by ourselves.

In watching Coleman's history we've been warned that no
one should have the effrontery to think they can truly make
themselves anew. The cruelty that it takes will be only one of
the many prices paid and in the end you get blindsided by the
much bigger world, 'the stranglehold of history that is one's own
time'. But without that dream of freedom you paradoxically
can't get true justification. If you don't strike out in your own
way, as all of us must to some degree to avoid submergence or

neediness, there would be little for others to judge at all. Only by, to some extent, being indifferent to the fear of disapproval can a rich connection be made. Without this indifference, however limited, you are forced by cramped motives and anxiety to shape and pander. And to control an audience too well is to render them impotent, where they can no longer provide worthwhile judgement. We need the other's judgement to be given as freely as possible, and the urge in ourselves to be free brings with it the ability to tolerate the lack of control we have over how others see us.

5

The last judgement

When singer Amy Winehouse's troubled life was played out on the big screen through the documentary film *Amy* it was an affront in particular to her father Mitch Winehouse, who discovered that he was wadded into his daughter's story as a 'money-grabbing, attention-seeking father who wasn't there'. He protested vigorously, 'Amy wouldn't want that, because Amy knows that is not the truth.'[1] The Winehouse family as a whole distanced themselves from the film claiming that it was 'unbalanced' and 'misleading', while the filmmakers countered that the story they told was a 'reflection of our findings' from 100 interviews and was approached with 'total objectivity'.

Whatever the merits of the film and the merits of the claim that it was a fair reflection of Amy Winehouse's life, it seems clear that 'total objectivity' is not available. The better question is whether the descriptive net in which they snared Amy Winehouse's life was created with sufficient care. Famous people are judged in a very public way and it is inevitable that judgements on their lives as a whole will be distorted. These distortions take many forms. In some cases, their fame condenses down to a trope or single idea: James Dean as rebellious youth, Mother Teresa as a saint, and so on. These compressions, even when expanded in biopics, inevitably offer up a version of a life that can't be the whole story. As Cary Grant once said, 'Everyone wants to be Cary Grant. Even I want to be Cary Grant.' Read Christopher Hitchens on Mother Teresa and very quickly you see that, as with so many versions of public lives, it is not nearly that simple.

The idea of a life judged in the round is as impossible as it is irresistible. The problem is not just to do with compression. It is also to do with what it takes to tell a coherent tale. Kierkegaard observed that life is lived forwards but only understood backwards. But this formulation promises a level of understanding, a level of narrative certainty, that cannot go hand in hand with accuracy.

There is thus a trade-off to be faced between telling an accurate story and telling a coherent (not to mention entertaining) one. We enjoy the narrative arc that gives shape to a life, but we can see that it has to be confected to a degree that renders the actual liver of that life somewhat inscrutable.

However 'objective' the filmmakers of *Amy* felt they were, there is nevertheless a major creative rendering, through compression, filtering and selection, and the demands of narrative that mean Amy Winehouse's portrayed life must in many ways depart from the whole story. And yet we want the story told anyway.

Telling tales

In order to try to 'know' people, some psychologists place individuals into a blend of particular circumstances that range from differences in biology, individual experience and cultural socialization that mark out their uniqueness. The personality researcher Dan McAdams's three-level model of personality[2] is a good example of this. He has distilled research across many fields in psychology to describe how getting to know someone is to see them on three levels, namely the *social actor*, the *motivated agent* and finally the *autobiographical author*.

The first level, that of the actor, describes your temperament and consists of *dispositional traits*. Over the last twenty years or so personality theorists have converged on what is known in the trade as 'The Big Five' personality traits. These are:

Extroversion: gregariousness, social dominance, enthusiasm, reward-seeking behaviour

Neuroticism: anxiety, emotional instability, depressive tendencies, negative emotions

Conscientiousness: industriousness, discipline, rule abidance, organization

Agreeableness: warmth, care for others, altruism, compassion, modesty

Openness: curiosity, unconventionality, imagination, receptivity to new ideas

These are general traits on which we all differ to some degree, and ones that operate across our lives influencing how we respond emotionally and cognitively to experiences in general. In his assessment of Donald Trump, for example, McAdams sees a man who has:

> sky-high *extraversion* (suggesting emotional exuberance and social dominance) and rock-bottom *agreeableness* (suggesting a decided *lack* of empathy, caring, kindness and altruism). Especially rare among people seeking public office, this combustible combination produces a social actor who is explosive, threatening and unpredictable.[3]

While traits seem to say something about us, they offer, according to McAdams, little more insight than knowing a stranger. Descriptions of traits are disconnected from context and so don't yield enough rich detail that is particular to an individual. McAdams is making much of the differences between these levels that might well come under strain when we confront the messy overlapping ways in which we conduct ourselves in practice. But for the sake of exposition there is something useful in making the levels conceptually distinct even if this is somewhat idealized. The next level of knowledge, where we are seen as *agents* of our behaviour, are *characteristic adaptations* or *personal concerns* which are more conditional and contextualized than traits. These include goals and values which can be seen as moral strivings. Characteristic adaptations can change over lifetimes more easily than dispositional traits and tend to be more specific to individual contexts. McAdams on Trump again:

> Trump's impulsive temperament style dovetails with his central life goal – the narcissistic aim of promoting Donald Trump. Ever since he attended New York Military Academy for high school, Donald Trump has doggedly pursued a motivational agenda of expanding, extolling, displaying and adoring the self.

This level of knowledge provides more insight into a person than mere dispositional traits, but it still won't tell us enough. Then we have McAdams's third level, that of the *author* who tells *integrative life stories.* This narrative identity is the central theme of this chapter, both in terms of what stories explain about ourselves to each other, as well as the limits of those telling tales. These are the narratives that people construct to make sense of themselves, especially in a way that puts their values and beliefs into a coherent frame. Often these will explicitly describe how an individual has arrived at political and moral stances in their lives.[4]

Donald Trump's personal narrative according to McAdam is all about how the world is full of danger, and how you have to be ready to fight. Trump tells many stories to support this world-view, of which this is a typical example:

> Fred Trump (Donald's father) made a fortune building, owning, and managing apartment complexes in Queens and Brooklyn. On weekends, he would occasionally take one or

two of his children along to inspect buildings. 'He would drag me around with him while he collected small rents in tough sections of Brooklyn,' Donald recalls in *Crippled America*. 'It's not fun being a landlord. You have to be tough.' On one such trip, Donald asked Fred why he always stood to the side of the tenant's door after ringing the bell. 'Because sometimes they shoot right through the door,' his father replied.

All lives when told can be looked at through a telescope or a microscope, making them small and average or detailed and textured by turns. Stories, for all their limitations, are necessary if we are to make any sense of lives in the round. Our lives literally, after all, have beginnings, middles and ends. More than that, in a quest for meaning, stories offer reasons and focal points and morals and are able to hold our attention. Although a non-narrative discourse may be informative, only stories can be gripping. Only stories seize the mind, by forging links between the ordinary and the extraordinary. There is a six-word novel, often attributed to Hemingway, that shows this point better than I can tell it:

For sale: baby shoes, never worn.

A story offers up incongruous mixes of the normal and the abnormal and brings them together in a way that conjures up an answer to a question that reverberates through our lives, namely 'why?'. The 'why' in question addresses human motives and requires an explanation with narrative shape. We only ask 'why' when something out of the ordinary happens. My mother tells a story about losing a contact lens in a bank many years ago. Several people were on the floor helping her to find it when they heard a scream. A new customer had walked in, saw people on the floor and assumed there was a holdup going on. The customer was fitting the unusual scene into a recognizable (if unlikely) narrative. She didn't just stand there baffled but cooked up the reason for why people were on their hands and knees. We always expect people to be doing things out of the ordinary 'for a reason'. Conventions and norms have a tendency to render action seemingly transparent and are thus relatively lacking in the need for interpretation. Breaches of expectation conjure up accounts that enable the unusual moment to be folded into a more intelligible story.

If I relate my early life in the Middle East and explain why we moved to the UK before I was ten, I can say I was born in Baghdad to a Jordanian engineer and contractor and an Irish teacher, and that the city seemed to them to be a good place to start a family and was full of career opportunities, which led to my parents having ten happy years there. But we left Iraq *because* Saddam Hussein had arrived on the scene and was going to make life intolerable for foreigners like my father. Later we were happy in Lebanon but left Beirut for Purley in south London *because* of the civil war in 1975 and the fact that my parents were shot at on the way home from a party in the wrong part of town. The parts of this sketchy story that sound like changes, or turning points, like the need to emigrate which requires a 'because', whereas 'ten happy years' in one city barely requires a note.

To frame a life in narrative terms is to find a way to give it meaning and significance. Many writers going back to Aristotle have commented that the narrative form submits to certain repeated elements and features. As an example of these efforts to form a typology of story-telling, the writer Christopher Booker spent most of his working life exploring the reoccurrence of just seven basic plots that seem to animate literature and other forms of story-telling like films in their various forms.[5] These forms can help give us some insight into the plot devices we might use in narrating our own lives. They are:

1   *Overcoming the monster*: this story form tells a tale of defeating some form of threat. The heroes we discussed above who show their skill this way are particularly satisfying as a story form. Booker compares the horror film *Jaws* with the Old English tale *Beowulf* to show their obvious parallels and how much in both cases we relish a tale of heroic victory over a fearsome enemy. But this drama can play out at many scales. When I started senior school in Purley I was occasionally bullied by a group of boys. One in particular was fond of sneering at me with the phrase 'Garlic A-rab'. I suffered the insult repeatedly during the first year of school. One afternoon, being taunted again by the physics lab, I punched him on his pointy chin. It wasn't much of a punch, but the bullying stopped after that. Monster overcome and another part of my biography narrated!

2   *Rags to riches*: where the impoverished protagonist gains fame and fortune. Sometimes this comes with a twist

where the new riches are then lost, but later regained along with a good dose of humble wisdom. And this story isn't fixated on the move from poverty to wealth specifically. It is about how the overlooked, the humble, the disregarded step into the limelight and gain applause. Think Cinderella or the phone-box transformation of Clark Kent into Superman. The story my father tells of his bankruptcy, with huge debts piling up after he left his business in Beirut, a city in ruins after the civil war in 1975, and having to rebuild the whole thing from scratch follows this pattern.

3 *The quest*: this form of story focuses on the pursuit of something of transformative value. In fables it can range from *Moby Dick* to the Holy Grail to *Saving Private Ryan*. The generic term used in Hollywood, often attributed to Hitchcock, is a 'MacGuffin'. And you can see how individual life stories might also work on this logic too. If you have a goal in life, pursue it and succeed, you have quite a story to tell. It doesn't have to be Francis Crick, John Watson and Rosalind Franklin discovering the double helix. It could equally be training for and running the London Marathon.

4 *Voyage and return*: this is a highly recognizable form: voyagers like the crew of *Star Trek* or Ulysses head out on their adventures, encountering life-altering experiences and sometimes tribulations, and return home to tell the tale. For some people, there is a literal round the world trip to describe, but for many just recounting the

experience of going to university will take this form. This story genre is a familiar part of most of our life accounts – even if, for many of us, it doesn't amount to more than describing an event-filled holiday.

The next fifth and sixth plots are *comedy* and *tragedy*, which each cover a vast range of circumstances but differ in how they are resolved. Whether you picture someone dealing with a terrible loss and working their way through immense sadness and pain where something good may come of that even if there is no true redemption. Even if the circumstances lead to a disastrous outcome – think Othello and his fatal flaw of jealousy – you still have the shape of a compelling tale told. In comedy, the hardship and threat of tragedy are resolved or avoided with the lighter shades of absurdity or saving wit, often at the expense of the protagonist. The comedy is usually carrying an undertow of darkness enabling us to laugh at our many sources of pain. In a film like *Bridesmaids* we can see how the pain of criticism, rejection, confusion and loss of status is kept at bay with a constant stream of wise-cracking and loving, if often temporary, resolutions.

Booker's seventh plot device is *rebirth*. He says:

Early in our lives we come across a type of story unlike any other. In the form in which we first encounter it, in the stories of childhood, it usually centres around the familiar fairy-tale cast of young heroes and heroines, princes and princesses, who have fallen foul of dark enchanters, wicked witches or evil stepmothers. But this is not a conventional Rags to

Riches or Overcoming the Monster story. It contains a crucial ingredient that marks it out from either. (193)

This ingredient involves some kind of personal transformation: I was lost but now am found. There is a story of growth and improvement and of lessons learned, often the result of a loving act of redemption. Think of a childhood anxiety carried forward into adulthood which is eventually resolved, or come to terms with, through a process of reconciliation or the facing of a fear.

I've taken the time to describe Booker's attempt to summarize the seven basic plots[6] as a way to explore what is involved in story-telling in general and to see how it might apply in the way we account for ourselves when we narrate our own lives. Such narrative is important in our pursuit of good judgement by offering episodes that enable us, directly or indirectly, to convey that we are nice and in control. Booker recognizes that there are variations on these basic themes and that many stories combine several of them in one go. I like the fact that there is something artificial about this typology, because it reminds us that story-telling is never a simple matter of telling the whole story. It is worth understanding that for a tale to be engaging it needs to be artfully conceived and must submit to principles of narration if it is to be interesting or even believable – if it is to be capable of being judged at all. In an effort to give our life stories narrative coherence, we need to punctuate them with episodes and focal points. We need to create dilemmas and resolutions, events and 'what happened next' for a tale to be worth telling.

What is more, I need to be able to say that these things are part of my biography even though they feel so long ago and are based so much on retellings rather than actual memories that I wonder what my relationship is to the young boy I'm describing. He is me, and he is not. The philosopher Alasdair Macintyre argues that the self is not a single, simple entity. Instead, you are the protagonist of a story that begins with birth and ends with death, which means that you can be held to account to explain the actions and choices that make up this story of your life.[7] If you cannot explain yourself in this way, we begin to doubt that you are who you say you are. This in turn requires that you are responsible for making your account intelligible. My telling must line up with the accounts other people have of any of my actions, and so my telling of the tale must line up with theirs.

We value continuity. We like to frame our stories as leading naturally along a narrative path where there is some link between past and future which sits somewhere between reality and fiction. Wittgenstein, in a different context, offers a useful metaphor:

We find that what connects all the cases of comparing [i.e. the use we make of the word 'comparing'...] is a vast number of overlapping similarities, and as soon as we see this, we feel no longer compelled to say that there must be some one feature common to them all. What ties the ship to the wharf is a rope, and the rope consists of fibres, but it does not get its strength from any fibre which runs through it from one end to the other, but from the fact that there is a vast number of fibres overlapping.[8]

This means when we explain changes and apparent inconsistencies we set about unweaving existing stories and replacing them with new ones. The person who states early in life 'I'm no good at maths' gets replaced gradually by the one who says 'I'm a keen stock market investor'. Often to lose a story is risky business, so we'd rather cling on. Give it the weight of meaning, and give it a taken-for-granted quality. But as soon as we intuit (or someone shows us) that there is no one doing the granting, that so much is our own, accidental, work we can't but help see the story fade. We have to allow for the unpredictable effect on us of our histories – our desires have been shaped by forces that are incredibly hard to see and challenge.

A central feature of autobiographical recall is to do with emotion. Maya Angelou once said she had learned that people, 'will forget what you said, people will forget what you did, but people will never forget how you made them feel'. And this insight is to some extent true of our reflections on our own lives; we tend to remember how things felt, whether bad, exciting or embarrassing. Once the emotional weather of the episode has been accessed, we must work in building up the story convincingly, one that is layered over those feelings so as to justify the emotional response itself and then find the appropriate words to explain it in retrospect. The confident, those who remember an emotion that is based on pride or conveys strength, remember more and more details, embellishing the story to reinforce the point. The less confident, plagued by emotion that is less flattering, such as shame, tend to recount less and less and leave their account vague enough to protect them in the mist.

My own version of how I went from Catholic to atheist during my teenage years has a certain rational-sounding sequence when told in retrospect, even if the underlying emotions are a truer reflection of what happened. The rational story goes like this: first, I remember doubting the Pope's right to kiss the tarmac at airports of poor countries in South America that were condemned to increased child mortality rates because of the Church's views on abortion. This then meant I shouldn't think so much in terms of Catholicism, but more generally of myself as Christian. But then I remember wondering why particular religions are so highly correlated with geography (not many Shintoists in Croydon at that time, while only six per cent of Jordanians were Christian) which seemed to me to make the idea of having one particular religion absurdly contingent on time and place. But then why not generalize to believing in a God without any particular religious affiliation? Well, this made sense until I discovered Bertrand Russell's *Why I Am Not a Christian* which carefully and convincingly demolished any reason to keep God in the picture, and secured me in my atheism ever since.

I'd like to say the rest is history, but I know it can't have been that simple and orderly. I'm rather more certain of the mix of feelings I had at that formative time in my life. The worry and anxiety that came from doubting what I'd taken to be true before that point; and the sense of how disappointed and anxious my still-Catholic mother would be. I cringe to think of the embarrassment of meeting Father Rochford, to whom I'd given my final confession a few days before, the moment I bumped into him in the music centre at school – he and I knew what I'd said in the supposedly anonymous confessional, and this created a deep discomfort in me. I remember the feeling of exhilaration that came from thinking that I could make my own mind up about something so important. I remember how angry I got with some religious friends about their views on homosexuality. However rational and coherent my official version, I know that cannot be how it really happened. But I'm more sure of the emotions involved and how easy it is to fit the explaining words on to those feelings retroactively. But since all I have now are my retellings of this transition from belief to non-belief, the official version will need to be the story I stick with. Like remembering a holiday from the photos you took rather directly from the experience, we are lost in versions that at least approximate how it felt at the time. For these reasons we should take well-honed accounts of how things happened with a pinch of salt, and know that our judgements of each will be trading to some extent on unreliable evidence. Even the teller of the story has limited access to what exactly happened at the time.

If we can't be trusted with our own recountings of individual episodes or focal points in our lives, how much less reliable are others in telling stories about us? Amy Winehouse's life has been presented back to us after her death, and her family reject the account. This is a particular hazard for the well-known. Most people don't have to wrestle with the interpretations of filmmakers and biographers. We barely make it into the category of 'also dead'. This phrase was used by Donatella Moss in *The West Wing* when she realized her significance in the pecking order of the US administration if there was a violent incident on a diplomatic trip. The news report she realized would say 'Deputy White House Chief of Staff Josh Lyman (her boss) was tragically killed today by a terrorist bomb. Also dead, Diane Moss.' The 'also dead' being such an afterthought they may not even get their name printed correctly, if at all.

While normal lives are not editorialized in a film like *Amy*, most people will have a funeral at which some attempt is made to judge their life as a whole and to identify the qualities and experiences that give that life its distinctiveness. While famous people are open to the distortions that come from needing compression and drama, everyday lives are also distorted at funerals, but often for a different reason. It is a final judgement which errs on the side of kindness, usually because everyone there is grieving, humbled by finitude and at the very least would not wish to 'speak ill of the dead'.

Everyday lives, when they end, start to look somewhat blameless and draw us into reverence for a life seen whole. And understandably so. You may recall a well-known advert for the John Lewis department store a few years ago which showed a baby growing up into an elderly woman. Along the way, we see the turning points in her life. The playing child turns into a schoolgirl, who turns into a young woman. We see her getting married, having children, and then grandchildren, etc. – all played out against the schmaltzy 'She's Always a Woman to Me' by Billy Joel. And cliché and generic and conventional and anonymous as this story is, there is something moving about seeing this notional 'everywoman's' finite life portrayed in this way. In that simple advert, what Joni Mitchell called 'The Circle

Game', is played out in one minute and thirty-one seconds, to advertise a department store, and yet the video has been watched nearly two million times – along with much emotionally expressive commentary.

Biopics, obituaries and funeral orations create more narrative than a lived life can truly yield, and so tend to round off and recast a life. My judgement of your life story is constrained by what you have chosen to put in, emphasize, or indeed to leave out. To fully judge a life, you'd need something like the map in Borges' short story 'On Exactitude in Science', which is based on the notion that the most accurate mapping that can be done of any terrain is to use a ratio of one to one; that is, where the map is the size of thing that it maps. Whoever writes an obituary has an angle and a word count to manage.[9]

When we try to capture the whole of our lives in these nets of narrative, the various features of conventional story-telling tend, in the process of simplification, to render textured lives vanilla smooth. At the end of the film *Saving Private Ryan*, we see the eponymous Ryan with his large extended family at the gravestone of the man who saved his life in the Second World War over 50 years before. The officer (played by Tom Hanks), who died while saving Private Ryan's life, leaves the latter with one phrase ringing through the rest of his life: 'Earn it!' And this is why Ryan turns to his wife and asks through tears, whether he has been a good man, as though such a big question can have a short answer.

But these bleached, saccharine treatments won't really do. We know that our lives are seasoned with more complexity than that. The irreverent writers who needed a last laugh help us to see life in a less sanctified or coherent way. Oscar Wilde saying 'This wallpaper and I are fighting a duel to the death. Either it goes or I do' or Groucho Marx's suggestion for his own epitaph, 'Excuse me, I can't stand up' help us to not feel dwarfed by the immensity and the attendant awed tones that death conjures up.[10] These writers are telling us not about death *per se*; they are giving us a glimpse into how they lived their individual lives.

If funerals give us the poignant vantage point of seeing the rope of a life laid out from beginning to end, we should be wary that the life thus stretched out is thus rendered too clean and straight. There is no getting away from telling stories, but not all stories need to be so simple.

Learning from literature

James Wood, the literary critic, quotes Walter Benjamin in his essay 'The Story Teller': 'Death is the fire around which the readers warm their hands.'[11] For Wood, death provides a vantage point from which a certain omniscience is possible, generating the story-teller's authority over the complete life thus described and therefore makes their story transmissible. You can say, for instance, that the protagonist only experienced true love twice in her life.

He says this loose packaging is the usefulness of fiction and points out how novels link experienced and remembered happenings, or instances and form. We can't do this in life as easily. We are lost in instances and unable to see the form until we look back. However, we can learn more about how to judge the texture of a life if we turn to literary novelists. The packaging of the story they offer while having narrative coherence can still allow for nuance and idiosyncratic detail. Unlike in simpler stories, we can see how significance, meaning and claims to posterity can emanate from a context of myriad complex details. Too much simplification renders a life too generic and too little leaves us at the mercy of un-narrated happenings. Margaret Atwood spoke well of how instances and form are in tension with each other:

> When you are in the middle of a story it isn't a story at all, but only a confusion; a dark roaring, a blindness, a wreckage of shattered glass and splintered wood; like a house in a whirlwind, or else a boat crushed by the icebergs or swept over the rapids, and all aboard powerless to stop it. It's only afterwards that it becomes anything like a story at all. When you are telling it, to yourself or to someone else.

To read fictional characters with their foibles and roles is to drift into a God's eye view of them. We look into their minds and convince ourselves we have 'monitoring powers'. As Wood puts it, we have the power 'to turn out the pocket of someone else's private thoughts and watch the loose change of error fall incriminatingly to the ground'. And yet because the characters are fictional, because the impact of their actions fall within the novel and are not directly interacting with real lives, we can judge them kindly. Wood goes further and says 'our scrutiny is always edging away from judgement (of the moralistic kind), toward proximity, fellow feeling, compassion, communion. We have the uncanny powers of the monitoring Jesus, but the humane insight of the forgiving Jesus ...' Woods may be over-claiming here. Whether this loving account is true of everyone we encounter through literature begs a question. Humbert Humbert preying on Dolores Haze in *Lolita* or O'Brien torturing Winston Smith in *1984* may not bring out our most loving sides after all. However, to judge a life, whether benignly or otherwise, is both a moral and aesthetic appraisal, meaning that a good reader resembles an art critic in certain ways, by noticing balance, drama, authenticity, phoniness, hollowness as well as the impact that was had on others. To judge well is, in this sense, to read well.

Attending to the details of other lives, doing what Wood calls 'serious noticing', is a good way to preserve an individual flame, and to judge more fairly, with more care, than a lazy and self-serving eye is inclined to do. In returning to Roth's *The Human Stain*, we might ask how should we judge Coleman Silk in the round? Do we forgive him or not for his relentless and sometimes brutal desire to escape? Who is to judge? Roth, it seems, wants Nathan Zuckerman, the narrator, to be the potent audience. So how does Nathan judge Coleman? Though he sees Coleman's weaknesses with 'monitoring powers' he is still, like the 'forgiving Jesus', more inclined to explain than to condemn. Nathan goes much further in fact and robustly defends the complex and flawed life of his friend. While he watches 'the loose change of error' fall to the ground, he resolutely refuses to find what he sees incriminating.

We learn early in the novel from Nathan that Coleman and Faunia have died. Their funerals are described later on, in a chapter called 'The Purifying Ritual'. As mentioned above, a funeral oration is a kind of summing up that of necessity traduces the complexity of the life lived, often by burying it and the person who lived it in homilies and sanctimony. And so it is for Coleman and Faunia, for whom death is the fundamental betrayer of their quiddity. As Nathan has it, 'Death intervenes to simplify everything. Every doubt, every misgiving, every uncertainty is swept aside by the greatest belittler of them all, which is death' (290). The funereal summaries put Coleman and Faunia's lives into the mouths of others, to reshape into a coherent story that de-stains them, with no right of reply. Faunia, for example, is reduced at her graveside to being a 'spiritual seeker' who loved the little herd of cows on the farm, and one who was warm and friendly who found nobility in cleaning toilets. Her crow voice is thereby silenced.

There is a grander purifying ritual for Coleman at his funeral. Nathan, the judge of his judges, tells us that many people packed in to watch a disloyal ex-colleague of his try to cleanse the story of Coleman Silk's reputational implosion, in an act of self-flagellation. 'Herb Keble was just another one out to kosher the record albeit in a bold, even interesting way, by taking the guilt upon himself, but the fact remained that he couldn't act when it mattered, and so I thought, on Coleman's behalf, fuck him.'

Nathan is antagonistically defensive of his closest friend, and recognizing that while a distant interpreter might argue for or against Coleman's freedom-hunting rebelliousness, it is none of their business.

> Was he merely being another American and, in the great frontier tradition, accepting the democratic invitation to throw your origins overboard if to do so contributes to the pursuit of happiness? Or was it more than that, or was it less? How petty were his motives? How pathological? And suppose they were both-what of it? And suppose they weren't – What of *that*? (334)

While Coleman was flawed and stained in many ways, his relationships with Nathan and Faunia redeem him to some extent in the eye of this reader. Through Nathan's eyes (as opposed to those of Coleman's cruelly rejected mother and brother) we can see him more sympathetically as a victim of harsh circumstance. 'Whipsawed by the inimical teeth of this world. By the antagonism that is this world' (316).

Nathan's judgement of Coleman is sympathetic and partly to do with a more personal understanding of Coleman's urge to be free. There is something wonderful about the uncritical and incomplete judgement of a loyal friend. In his book *On Friendship* the acutely perceptive philosopher Alexander Nehamas compares a friend to that of living metaphor. A living metaphor, like 'architecture is frozen music', is one in which you can always find more resonances, unlike a dead metaphor which descends into cliché and which can be accurately summarized. When someone 'kicks the bucket', it simply means that they have died. There is no more to say than that. Instrumental relationships have something of this fungible quality too. If you just spend time with someone because they cut your hair then they are to an extent interchangeable with someone else who can perform the same task. A true friend, like a living metaphor, or a work of art that matters has a unique and ineffable quality that requires perpetual and unique attention. 'Who you actually are makes a tremendous difference: like a living metaphor, you are irreplaceable.'[12] He extends the thought to say that 'Just as with metaphors we never fully know what their role in our life will be'. A close friendship is the opposite of being interchangeable and the possibilities of interpretation are never ending.

Nathan was lucky to find this quality of friendship late in his life. He had experimented with freedom in his own way, picturing himself, until his friendship with Coleman Silk, as one who escapes the rush and 'lives, away from all agitating entanglements, allurements and expectations apart, especially from one's own intensity' which means you have to 'organise the silence,... The encircling silence as your chosen source of advantage and your only intimate'. But this attempt at isolation, unwitnessed, is not enough for Nathan. He recognizes the limits of the urge to be free without the complicity of others, both for himself and his friend, 'the secret to living in the rush of the world with a minimum of pain is to get as many people as possible to string along with your delusions' (44).

Nathan is the one who can speak for Coleman in a way that reflects the particularity of his story. Roth, in presenting Nathan presenting Coleman to us, has conjured up what James Wood calls 'lifeness', including the unavoidable fact of unreliable narration. While lifeness may be the nearest thing to life, it is still not life itself. If Nathan can speak for Coleman and Roth can speak for Nathan with his God's eye point of view, who can speak for the rest of us? While we can have more compassion toward fictional characters, we are more likely to cast the first stone at real people because real people have real impacts on us and others, and a stronger or different kind of judgement is necessary. So even if literature can be seen as an empathy engine which helps to shape our communion with the 'other', there must be limits to empathy in real-world encounters and judgement is woven into our encounters with each other – whether we like it or not. But what we can learn from literature is a way to be more provisional in our judgements. To recognize contradictions, and to see, for example, how love and hate are operated by the same glands (as Graham Greene put it). Literature invites a kaleidoscopic view of each other in which we will be less cartoonish and more careful in our depictions.

In *The Ego Trick: What Does It Mean To Be You?*, the philosopher Julian Baggini interviews various experts to put together an image of the self that is less coherent and more accurate than one to which we are typically inclined. He says we tend to view ourselves as a pearl in a shell, enduring and solid. But this is the wrong metaphor to help us grasp what is going on. We are not a pearl inside a shell any more than we are a face under a mask, or even an actor going on and off stage, any more than a bare tree in winter is any more real than a tree in leaf. We seem to be more like an ongoing performance by a thronging company of players, all of whom take their turns without there being any special claim to an original, a fixed truth, a start or an end – even though across the mingling of the whole we may well discern themes and values.[13] Better to replace that pearly metaphor with the image of a bundle of thoughts, memories, ideas and versions changing through time. One of Baggini's interviewees, the philosopher Galen Strawson, appears to have a more extreme sense of discontinuity than most. He eschews the idea of a narrative self which he sees as an illusion to which he is not at all prone: 'There are people like me who just feel that they're effectively in the moment and they don't really think that the self that they are in the moment was there even a minute ago.' The heart of the Ego Trick is to keep the bundle under wraps and allow the narrative coherence of the pearl view to stand: 'the trick is to create something which has a strong sense of unity and singleness of form from what is actually a messy, fragmented sequence of experiences and memories, in a brain which has no control centre'.[14] This skill, of 'serious noticing', careful assessment and a willingness to revise judgements in light of what we learn anew can help strike the necessary balance between fidelity to the incoherence of lived experience and something more intelligible. However good we may be at pulling off this trick, we don't need to have the disorientating intuitions of a Galen Strawson to realize it is, however skilful played, a trick nevertheless.

Significance

It is poignant to read the poetry of Philip Larkin, who so feared and anticipated his own death, and wrote this into so much of his poetry, such as 'Aubade' or 'Continuing to Live'. All the more, in that we now know with a sad precision, in answer to his speculation, that he died at the age of sixty-three in Kingston upon Hull on 2 December 1985.

The poignancy goes beyond this God's eye view, however. Larkin didn't just fear his inevitable death, he also feared that in the end the life he had led would be insignificant. The ultra-social animal that we are has a deep need to feel judged well, but behind that preference is the need to be judged at all. This requires that we are significant enough in the eyes of others to merit their evaluation. In his poem 'Continuing to Live', Larkin pictures that final moment of retrospect, that 'green evening where [his] death begins', and imagines a reckoning where 'we half-identify the blind impress/All our behavings bear' – a time when you take stock of what you have and haven't done and understand its impact on the world and others. And when you do you will realize this 'lading list' is 'hardly satisfying/Since it applied to one man once,/And that one dying'. The implication is that significance will escape us in the end. Dust returns to dust and the blind impress fades from view. Think of Macbeth commenting after the death of Lady Macbeth how:

> Life's but a walking shadow, a poor player
> That struts and frets his hour upon the stage,

And then is heard no more. It is a tale
Told by an idiot, full of sound and fury,
Signifying nothing.[15]

The irony of course is that unlike so many lives that fade away in the way he describes, to one person once 'And that one dying', Larkin himself is remembered for having expressed this fear of insignificance, his life is a tale told by a poet, not an idiot, in such a way that has remained significant ever since.

Not everyone gets a biopic or even an 'also dead' (even with the wrong name printed), but there are times when ordinary lives turn filmic and become narrated too. Like funerals, weddings offer a similar stage where the marrying couple are unquestioned celebrities for that one day, and of whom speeches must be made and to whom attention must be paid. Guests feel singled out and lucky when the 'happy couple' talk to them. This is an example of the heightened and rare moments in a normal life when public narration is required. But most of the time our lives go by unheralded.

The small and subtle significance of our actions can be recovered of course, but this is a truth revealed through careful attention. George Eliot ended *Middlemarch* in a way which I have long found moving, with these words about the protagonist Dorothea, who lived life in a necessarily unheroic way in a small town:

But the effect of her being on those around her was incalculably diffusive: for the growing good of the world is partly dependent on unhistoric acts; and that things are not so ill with you and me as they might have been is half owing to the number who lived faithfully a hidden life, and rest in unvisited tombs.

In this Eliot was doing the work of quiet recovery that is so important in appreciating the subtle effects we can have on each other and the significance that results from their cumulative force. Saved by the all-seeing eye of the novelist, Dorothea's subtle significance is preserved. But normal audiences can rarely be expected to offer this quality of care. Eliot has a more tragic view of everyday judgement in which 'we are all of us born in moral stupidity, taking the world as an udder to feed our supreme selves'. The subtlety, care and attention we owe to each other 'has not yet wrought itself into the coarse emotion of mankind; and perhaps our frames could hardly bear much of it. If we had a keen vision and feeling of all ordinary human life, it would be like hearing the grass grow and the squirrel's heartbeat, and we should die of that roar which lies on the other side of silence'.

Without a caring and careful audience, what can the rest of us do to fight off this feeling of insignificance and futility in light of the more uncomprehending gaze? One option is known as the 'George Bailey technique' after the character played by James Stewart in Frank Capra's 1946 film *It's a Wonderful Life*. Near the end of the film we see George on his uppers on Christmas Eve, bankrupt, depressed and wanting to commit suicide because 'he's worth more dead than alive' thanks to his life insurance policy. But he sees a man apparently drowning in the river whom he saves. The man turns out to be George's guardian angel, Clarence Odbody. Clarence decides to show to George what the town would be like if he'd never been born. Of course, his effects on many aspects of the town are remarkably positive, or 'incalculably diffusive' in Eliot's words. It's a simple enough plot device, but is moving precisely because it overturns George's feeling of insignificance so neatly.

The story gives us a clue into tactics we can try to alleviate the burden of feeling insignificant. The reason this story works to overcome George's feeling of futility is not about counting blessings *per se*. Some have suggested that a way to appreciate your life is to keep a gratitude journal in which you list the things that make you thankful. But research shows this is of limited value. In his book *Redirect*, the psychologist Tim Wilson points out our proneness to the Pleasure Paradox. If we count our blessings too often, such as in a gratitude journal, the significance of the good news diminishes over the repeated retellings. It is far more effective to learn the true lesson of the George Bailey technique which is to imagine experiences or relationships that you value had never happened and how lucky you are that this sorry state of affairs never materialized. This makes the feeling of appreciation much stronger. Wilson comments that if you ask people to focus, for example, on their partners being out of their lives this 'made [their relationship] seem surprising and special again, and maybe a little mysterious – the very conditions that prolong the pleasure we get from the good things in life'.

We don't have guardian angels to reassure us of the importance of our lives, and there is presumably a limit to the pleasure to be had even from the George Bailey technique. We depend on the various real audiences we encounter and, as we have seen, they are quite fickle in their judgements. Wilson describes the asymmetry we experience when it comes to reflecting on positive or negative judgements. Say you are bedevilled by someone being harsh towards you. The best way to handle it is distancing yourself from the critique and recounting it as if it happened to someone else. If, on the other hand, it is a good experience then you can enjoy what he calls 'the pleasures of uncertainty'. This is a general issue of asymmetry between negative and positive judgement. If you are telling someone something nice, you can be vague. If you are telling them something critical, you need to be concrete and specific, taking care to focus on the sin rather than the sinner.

Another route to avoiding the fear of insignificance is to deny the significance of the judgement of others; in essence to try and ignore the feeling of being ignored. This was the path to freedom explored in the last chapter and much of the story of Coleman Silk's life. A less dramatic way to see this was suggested by the novelist Vikram Seth during his appearance on the radio programme *Desert Island Discs*. During the interview he mentioned an older woman he knew with a good approach to life and other people. She said that rather than spend so much of her time thinking about how other people think of *her*, she would instead focus on what *she* thought of other people. He decided to try and learn this lesson a little earlier in life.

There is something simple and powerful about this table-turning mental shift. And I'm sure it is good advice for those of us caught up too self-consciously in others' opinions. It is often observed that in later stages in life the anxiety about being judged declines. Jenny Joseph's poem 'Warning', which starts 'When I am an old Woman I shall wear purple', captures some of this rebellious spirit. Along with her purple clothes she will go out into the world and will 'gobble up samples in shops and press alarm bells/And run my stick along the public railings'. She will make up for the 'sobriety of [her] youth' and she will learn to spit. And then she ends the poem with a thought. Why wait? 'Maybe I ought to practice a little now' in the spirit of Vikram Seth learning not to wait until he's seventy before focusing more on what he thinks of others.

But there are limits to that hope as well, as we explored in the last chapter. We can't break too free of our potent audiences. A descent into eccentricity or just focusing overly much on what you think about other people and not at all about what people think of you is to suffer a slow disconnection from the sources of justification. To be too successful in this shift is to become isolated; no longer accountable to others' views and causing significance and meaning to thin out again. In any case, imagine a world where everyone succeeded in this view. We would all become judges, never judged. This path involves never risking the pain of being ill judged and never having the chance of feeling justified by the same token.

Of course, to reckon with judgement, to care what other people think, is to submit yourself to regular disappointments. We need to recognize that there is much outside our current control, and that we will be judged for these things on occasion, and that this will feel excruciatingly unfair. We have seen, in this book, much to feel discouraged about in the nature of human judgement. Evolutionary pressures don't really care whether or not we are designed to be happy and flourishing. Our tendencies were selected to enable reproductive success, which leads to a potentially tragic view of ourselves as doomed to repeat the same failings. Prone to self-deception, hypocrisy, self-righteousness and bias that make our judgements of each other as unreliable as they are self-serving, we are controlled by Haidt's unconscious elephant lurching this way and that, and there's very little we can do about it.

The world is filled with bad judgement and there is a great inequality that frequently reproduces itself. As with financial inequality, we can even see what's known as the Matthew effect, where those who are already rich in good judgement receive yet more (the foibles of the well-regarded forgiven as eccentricity) and those with less more prone to condemnation, in what can feel like virtuous and vicious circles. The judgement of others is as powerful as it is unregulated. And where the unfairness becomes excruciating we need on occasion to say 'It's not my fault' or 'I don't care' or indeed 'No one will ever truly understand me.'

Ultimately, we have little control over how we are judged by potent audiences. They would not be potent if we had that much control. We are not in a position to occupy neutral ground, and if you think you are, the literature on implicit bias will make sobering reading. What we can do is recognize that our judgements will often be wrong, partial and self-serving. So, make those judgements but don't stop there. Recognize they are

provisional and need revising in light of more evidence. This is
the thing we don't do nearly enough. This is why John Maynard
Keynes has to ask us, 'when the facts change I change my mind,
what do you do?'. Well, I know what I do. Like many of us in today's
world of echo chambers and club culture, it is hard to escape the
bubble, the digital hall of mirrors that can only reflect our own
crooked timber. So I get comfortable in my judgements and start
to see them as taken-for-granted facts of my social world. I don't
think enough like some novelists or anthropologists, what the
philosopher Richard Rorty called agents of love. These agents of
love are the counter to the agents of justice in any healthy society.
The agents of justice are the purveyors of standard treatments
considering us all equal before the law, a notionally blind justice
that does not differentiate but lays out disinterested evaluations
of people irrespective of their particular circumstances. This is all
very well in theory but does not recognize that many particulars
of our situations, whether physical, historical or social, mark
us off from each other. Agents of justice are blinkered without
agents of love. The part of us which dispenses justice needs to
be equally prone to a loving susceptibility to the particular. The
agents of love are the ones who bring the once unaccepted from
the margins into the purview of the agents of justice. There are
laws against discrimination on the basis of race, gender and age
which required agents of love to give voice to forms of suffering
that had hitherto been silenced or ignored. The agents of love
have this susceptibility and are willing to render the unfamiliar
familiar and to complicate the story. The literary novelists provide
many worked through accounts that exhibit this tendency, from

which we can learn. Wide-eyed, seriously noticing, open to being surprised, they help to avoid 'the slow death we deal to the world by the sleep of our attention' as James Wood puts it.[16]

However good an agent of love you might be, you will, like Nathan Zuckerman, know the limit of this ambition. 'For all that the world is full of people who go around believing they've got you or your neighbour figured out, there really is no bottom to what is not known. The truth about us is endless. As are the lies' (315).

Robert Hass's poem 'Privilege of Being' tells a story of a loving couple in their intimacy realizing how irreducible singular and unknowable they must ultimately be to each other. She says to him:

> *I woke up feeling so sad this morning because I realized*
> *that you could not, as much as I love you,*
> *dear heart, cure my loneliness,*
> wherewith she touched his cheek to reassure him
> that she did not mean to hurt him with this truth.
> And the man is not hurt exactly,
> he understands that life has limits, that people
> die young, fail at love,
> fail of their ambitions.

There is pathos in this view, which can be read either as bleak or as redemptive. Something in that ambivalence is captured in the psychoanalyst Jacques Lacan's observation that love involves 'giving something you don't have to someone who doesn't want it'.

I was surprised to hear my daughters describing how it was possible to feel truly loved by a relative who didn't really know them individually, but loved each one of them in a tangible, quite specific way nevertheless. I was surprised because I had tended to think of how love depends on eliminating the gap of knowledge between people. But this kind of intimacy, that feeling of knowing and being known in return, is so fleeting and elusive it is nothing like enough to be the basis for something as powerful and redemptive as love or to support many other types of deeply rewarding relationship.

I've learned in writing this book that it is no failure in the end to recognize that no one will ever truly understand you. Even to see that the attempt to understand is not only ultimately fruitless but in some ways is undermining of the connection it claims to seek. The implication of God's eye control that comes from truffling out 'the truth' sits ill, at times, with a need to accept our ignorance and be accepting of the sheer otherness of the people we claim to know. Not even you fully understand you. And since my judgement of you will never be a complete or accurate story I must realize that approaching understanding of you, in some ways, keeps it away. Like walking toward an ever-receding horizon, I can approach without, in some crucial way, ever getting truly close.

But this deferral of understanding, this mutual ignorance, creates a certain kind of hope. Despite it we can and will judge each other, as through a glass darkly, but in a state of constant anticipation. My reach *should* exceed my grasp. This is a recipe for revisiting our judgements in the knowledge that they will always be partial and a call to be humble in the face of our self-righteous certainties which come too quick and often. And acknowledging this lack of knowledge, the inevitable limits of scrutiny, can be enabling in a different way. In these lacunae each of us can project ourselves toward a better version. Rather than feeling an uncomfortable gap between the stories we tell ourselves and those others tell about us, we can perhaps use these gaps to provide elbow room enough to transform them beyond wishful thinking. If everyone thinks I'm kinder than I feel I am, I can focus on that gap and try to close it in future. This way we may develop new habits and virtues and interests over time, rather than feeling stuck in a preordained pearly truth. The gaps in knowledge can offer such tentative hope. That's how the light gets in, after all.

For good or ill, the fact that no one will really know you is unavoidable. We should remember the tattoo Coleman Silk had received long before on that dreadful night of shame and self-recrimination during his time in the navy. For his closest friend Nathan, this was 'a tiny symbol, if one were needed of all the million circumstances of another fellow's life, of that blizzard of details that constitute the confusion of a human biography. A tiny symbol to remind me that our understanding of other people must always be at best slightly wrong'.

No, we can't stop our unreliable judging, nor will we always be judged fairly or accurately ourselves. But we can notice the *way* we judge each other, and notice when we have stopped noticing too. If we can do that, then we will learn more about the people in our lives and learn more, if not everything, from them in return.

Acknowledgments

The initial idea for this book was suggested to me by Steven Gerrard, the publisher of my previous book *Intimacy*, during a drink at the Frankfurt book fair, and evolved from there on through conversations with my ever-supportive agent Will Francis. Over the years since then it has benefitted from comments from a range of people. I'm grateful for feedback on specific chapters from Paul Peters, Matt Flinders and Tom Chatfield – thanks to Tom in particular, who not only commented extensively and insightfully but also inspired the subtitle. Special thanks go to those who went the extra mile and read the whole script and commented in detail throughout, including Kate Buchanan, Dave Clarke, Sam Grove, Mark Lattimer, Nael Marar, Leith Marar, Neil Sentance and Kiren Shoman.

I'm hugely grateful to Liza Thompson, my editor at Bloomsbury, who commissioned me following a talk I gave in which I'd mentioned that my previous books had involuntarily shifted publishers due to a company sale. She has been a careful and insightful guide since and has helped improve the book in many ways, usually over an 'old school' publishing lunch. I've also had remarkable enthusiasm and support from Nigel

Newton who has championed my work for years now. Also at Bloomsbury I have to thank Frankie Mace, Rachel Nicholson, Maria Hammershoy, Beth Williams, Rebecca Willford at Integra and also Emily Gibson for her skilled and observant copy editing.

Finally I'm most grateful of all to my family. Kate, Anna, Ellie and Charlotte: Thank you for indulging me in repetitious conversations that have roamed across every part of the book, and for lovingly tolerating countless intrusions into weekends and holidays with (mainly!) good humour. I couldn't have written it without you.

Notes

Introduction

1   R. F. Baumeister, E. Bratslavsky, C. Finkenauer and K. D. Vohs, 'Bad is Stronger than Good', *Review of General Psychology*, 5 (2001): 323–70.

2   Leslie Farber, *Ways of the Will* (New York, 2000).

3   Adam Phillips, *Monogamy* (London, 1996), 7.

4   Abraham Maslow developed a theory of human motivation based on a hierarchy of needs. The most basic level needs are physiological, e.g. for food, water and safety. The next level is psychological, including friendship, love and prestige and finally the highest level is around self-fulfilment and self-actualization. His claim was that you don't tend to have higher level needs until the lower level ones have been met.

5   Erving Goffman, *Stigma: Notes on the Management of Spoiled Identity* (Harmondsworth, 1963), 128.

Chapter 1

1   Erving Goffman, *Interaction Ritual* (New Brunswick, 1967/2005), 33:

The human tendency to use signs and symbols means that evidence of social worth and of mutual evaluations will be conveyed by minor things, and these things will be witnessed, as will the fact that they have been witnessed. An unguarded glance, a momentary change of voice, an ecological position taken or not taken, can drench a talk with judgmental significance. Therefore, just as there is no occasion of talk in which improper impressions could not intentionally or unintentionally arise, so there is no occasion of talk so trivial as not to require each participant to show serious concern with the way in which he handles himself and the others present.

2 Woods acknowledges Ford Maddox Ford's use of this example on what he calls 'getting a character in'.

3 See Nancie George, 'How Social Pain Affects Your Mind and Body', *Everyday Health* (22 January 2015), www.everydayhealth.com/news/how-social-pain-affects-your-mind-body/.

4 Oliver Burkeman, *The Antidote* (Edinburgh, 2012), 25.

5 Mark Leary, *The Curse of the Self: Self-Awareness, Egotism, and the Quality of Human Life* (New York, 2007), 77.

6 Quoted in Ephraim H. Mizruchi, *The Substance of Sociology* (New York, 1973), 200.

7 Until children develop what's known as a 'theory of mind' – the ability to see things from another's point of view, and crucially the ability to think about what other people think about them – these emotions would make no sense.

8 Goffman, *Interaction Ritual*, 111.

9 Brené Brown, 'Listening to Shame', *TED Talk* (16 March 2012), https://www.ted.com/talks/brene_brown_listening_to_shame.

10 John Sabini and Maury Silver, *Emotion, Character and Responsibility* (New York, 1998), 21.

11 Adam Phillips, 'Against Self-Criticism', *London Review of Books*, 5 March 2015.

12 So, shame and guilt are in fact mutually compatible and sometimes intimately associated. A single action can elicit both. John Rawls in *A Theory of Justice* asks you to:

imagine for example someone who cheats or gives in to cowardice and then feels both guilty and ashamed. He feels guilty because he has acted contrary to his sense of right and justice. By wrongly advancing his interest, he has transgressed the rights of others, and his feelings of guilt will be more intense if he has ties of friendship and association to the injured parties. He expects others to be resentful and indignant at his conduct, and he fears their righteous anger and the possibility of reprisal. Yet he also feels ashamed because his conduct shows that he has failed to achieve the goal of self-command, and he has been found unworthy of his associates upon whom he depends to confirm his sense of his own worth. He is apprehensive lest they reject him and find him contemptible, an object of ridicule. In his behavior, he has betrayed a lack of the moral excellences he prizes and to which he aspires. (Rawls 1971, 445).

13 Steven Pinker, *The Stuff of Thought: Language as a Window into Human Nature* (London, 2008).

14 Fiske describes a fourth relationship type, known as 'market pricing'. He claims we evolved to learn the first three, which all come naturally to us in different settings, but the fourth is a more recent phenomenon that occurs in post-industrial market-based societies and involves instrumental assessments of pure utility, and is something we are not well adapted to handling intuitively.

15 M. Morgan et al. (2006). 'Interactions of Doctors with the Pharmaceutical Industry', *Journal of Medical Ethics* 32(10), 559–63.

16 P. M. Lewinsohn, W. Mischel, W. Chaplain and R. Barton (1980). 'Social Competence and Depression: The Role of Illusory Self-Perceptions?' *Journal of Abnormal Psychology*, 89, 203–12.

17 And many of them argue that the result of the Brexit referendum in the UK was an example where the expressive trumps the instrumental.

18 Sam Selvon, *The Lonely Londoners* (London, 1956), 25.

19 Kate Fox, *Watching the English: The Hidden Rules of English Behaviour* (London, 2005), 92.

20 'Saying uncovers the one that speaks, ... The unblocking of communication ... is accomplished in saying ... It is in the risky

uncovering of oneself, in sincerity, the breaking up of inwardness and the abandon of all shelter, exposure to traumas, vulnerability' (Emmanuel Levinas, *Otherwise Than Being, or, Beyond Essence* (Dordrecht, 1998), 48–9).

21 Richard Feynman, *Surely You're Joking, Mr. Feynman!* (New York, 1997), 60.

22 Charles Percy Snow, *The Two Cultures* (Cambridge 2001 [1959]).

23 Clifford Geertz, who developed Ryle's insight about thick description comments that 'Man is an animal suspended in webs of significance he himself has spun. I take culture to be those webs and the analysis of it to be therefore not an experimental science in search of law but an interpretive one in search of meaning' (*The Interpretation of Cultures* (New York, 1973)).

24 Mark Leary, *Self Presentation* (Colorado, 1995), 165.

25 Leary tested people described as 'mavericks' versus those that could be described as 'needy'. He put them each in a room and got them to speak into a microphone about themselves. They could see a rating from invisible listeners tracking between one and seven as to whether the listener wanted to interact with them. The ratings were rigged and the outcome revealed that everyone cares, whether maverick or needy. Leary's conclusion was 'the sociometer operates at a non conscious and pre-attentive level to scan the social environment for any and all indications that one's relational value is low or declining'. (Ibid, 78)

26 Tesser Self Evaluation Maintenance Theory sets out ways we manage to avoid having to compete for self-esteem in our 'top domains' with those near and dear. 'Our choices of friends and partners, and how we react to those friends' and partners' successes, are affected by our own desire to feel good about ourselves'. (Leary, *Curse of the Self*, 115.)

27 As Sabini and Silver (1998) explain, 'sincerity (authenticity, genuineness, phoniness, hollowness, etc.) is both moral and aesthetic'. When we started it appeared as if enacted roles and genuine feelings were necessarily in opposition. Since sincerity was a matter of feeling,

of conscious contents, of impulses and tugs, any model that dealt with rules, standards, manipulated impressions – social constructions – could not approach sincerity. We have argued instead that sincerity, even sincerity as seen as a match between feelings and avowals, requires rules, standards, and even manipulations – the constructed stuff. (64).

Chapter 2

1 As was presciently predicted by the psychologist Herb Simon in the 1970s.

2 S. D. Reicher and S. A. Haslam, 'The Politics of Hope: Donald Trump as an Entrepreneur of Identity', in M. Fitzduff (ed.), *Why Irrational Politics Appeals* (Santa Barbara, CA, 2017), 25–40.

3 R. Harré, *Social Being*, 2nd edn (Oxford, 1993).

4 Jonathan Haidt, *The Righteous Mind* (London, 2012), 54.

5 Though you could question the direction of travel: Does a concern for a good reputation encourage us to act morally, or is the causal arrow pointing the other way (as we might like to think)? Either way, when it comes to reputations the word 'good' tends to have this moral tone and to go with trustworthiness. We are accordingly extremely sensitized to cheats and free-riders.

6 NHS Choices, 'Alcohol "a Direct Cause of Seven Types of Cancer"', www.nhs.uk/news/2016/07July/Pages/alcohol-a-direct-cause-of-seven-types-of-cancer.aspx.

7 Aronson identified this in *The Social Animal*. Other social psychologists have come up with a clunky neologism for this combination, calling it 'beneffectance', a compound of benevolence and effectiveness.

8 Steven Pinker, *How the Mind Works* (London, 1997), 421–3.

9 Susan T. Fiske, Amy J. C. Cuddy and Peter Glick (2006). 'Universal Dimensions of Social Cognition: Warmth and Competence', *TRENDS in Cognitive Sciences* 11(2), 77–83, http://fidelum.com/wp-content/uploads/2013/10/Warmth-Competence-2007.pdf.

10 The name Gray Matter, colleagues of mine will be amused to know, came from combining the names of the two founders, namely White and Schwartz, meaning 'black' in German.

11 Michel de Montaigne, *The Complete Works of Montaigne: Essays, Travel Journals, Letters*, ed. and trans. Donald C. Frame (Stanford, CA, 1958), I: 28, 'Of Friendship', 142.

12 Jonathan Haidt distinguishes between 'admiration' and 'elevation', saying that the former is inspired by non-moral excellence, i.e. competence, while the latter is inspired by moral excellence: Sara B. Algoea and Jonathan Haidt (2009). 'Witnessing Excellence in Action: the "Other-Praising" Emotions of Elevation, Gratitude, and Admiration', *Journal of Positive Psychology* 4(2), 105–27, www.ncbi.nlm.nih.gov/pmc/articles/PMC2689844/.

13 This is in fact a parody of the actual Venn diagram created by Anna Faherty after a talk I gave to her students: 'Love and Money: It's all about the Author for Sage', https://kingstonpublishing.wordpress.com/2011/11/06/love-and-money-its-all-about-the-author-for-sage/.

14 Jonathan Haidt, et al. (2007). 'The New Synthesis in Moral Psychology', *Science* 316, 998, http://www.unl.edu/rhames/courses/current/readings/new-synthesis-haidt.pdf.

15 Milan Kundera, *Slowness* (London, 1998), 44.

Chapter 3

1 Clifford Geertz, *The Interpretation of Cultures* (New York 1973), 45.

2 You can take the test here and see for yourself: https://implicit.harvard.edu/implicit/takeatest.html.

3 S. J. Spencer, C. M. Steele and D. M. Quinn (1999). 'Stereotype Threat and Women's Math Performance', *Journal of Experimental Social Psychology*, 35, 4–28.

4 American Psychological Association, 'Stereotype Threat Widens Achievement Gap', 15 July 2006, http://www.apa.org/research/action/stereotype.aspx.

5 'Iris Bohnet on Discrimination and Design', *Social Science Bites* (interview), 10 May 2016, https://www.socialsciencespace.com/2016/05/iris-bohnet-on-discrimination-and-design/.

6 Daniel Kahneman, *Thinking Fast and Slow* (London, 2011).

7 Daniel Kahneman and Amos Tversky, 'Judgement under Uncertainty', *Science* 27 Sep 1974.

8 Celia Moore and Francesco Gino (2013), 'Ethically Adrift: How Others Pull Our Moral Compass from True North, and How We Can Fix It', *Research in Organizational Behavior*, 33, 53-77.

9 Jonathan Haidt, *The Righteous Mind: Why Good People are Divided by Politics and Religion* (London, 2012), 61 cites the work of Chenbo Zhong who also showed that the reverse is true too, asking people to recall their own or even to write down descriptions of others' moral transgressions will be more inclined to want to wash. He calls this the 'Macbeth effect'.

10 The evolutionary account suggests we've developed these reflexes so as to know who to trust and therefore who we can cooperate with. This may be a species of just-so story, but even if valid it doesn't mean this is what is going on in our minds now. An evolved preference that might have served a purpose long ago might explain how it arrived, like a sweet tooth once helped survival by motivating people to find scarce sugar and fats, but long after that is widely available and no longer meets that need. For evolutionists, the original (distal) motivation to behave a certain way (such as having sex for procreation) can over time become disconnected from that original purpose while still being a strong tendency for recent (proximal) motivation. So, moral intuitions persist even if we aren't in a constant state of anxiety about whether

we will be able to trade or cooperate successfully with other group members. The same goes for cultural evolution. We have come a long way from shaking hands to show that we aren't concealing weapons, but the practice continues nevertheless.

11 Robert McCrum, 'A Conversation with Philip Roth', *The Guardian*, 1 July 2011, www.theguardian.com/books/2001/jul/01/fiction. philiproth1.

12 See Martha C. Nussbaum, *Hiding from Humanity: Disgust, Shame and Law* (Princeton, NJ, 2004).

13 An amendment to the UK Local Government Act 1988, which was eventually repealed in 2000.

14 L. Kass (1997). 'The Wisdom of Repugnance', *New Republic* 216(22), http://www.public.iastate.edu/~jwcwolf/336/KASS.pdf.

15 Known now as the Social Intuitionist Model.

16 *The New Republic*, 'The Stupidity of Dignity', 28 May 2008, https:// newrepublic.com/article/64674/the-stupidity-dignity.

17 In recent years Haidt and his colleagues have since proposed a sixth foundation, namely liberty vs oppression. This is strongly seen in the libertarian tendency to resist constraints on freedom. It often pulls in the opposite direction to the authority foundation and wants to punish bullies and to resist oppression. Haidt et al. have come up with these candidates for moral foundations but recognize that through further research more could be established or some might end up being combined, but they stick with the idea that there are many.

18 This account of our moral foundations is rooted in the insights of anthropologist Richard Shweder, who countered the peculiarly Western notion of morality being bound up with the individual to recognize that in most places and most times human beings have had a far wider array of moral groundings. By contrasting individualist with collectivist cultures, he suggested that the former value an ethic of autonomy, which is clearly recognizable in the West and is to do with individual harms and rights, whereas the latter offer up an ethic

of community which emphasizes duty and following communal will as well as an ethic of divinity which invites you to treat your body as your temple, emphasizing the sacred and the pure. This tripartite distinction of autonomy, community and divinity applies across cultures to varying degrees with autonomy most pronounced in a minority of cultures, mainly in the West.

19 Joe Henrich, Steve Heine and Ara Norenzayan (2010). 'The Weirdest People in the World?', *Behavioral and Brain Sciences* 33 (2–3), 61–83.

20 There is a popular argument that we should in fact only use the first two moral foundations in judging others. According to this liberal view morality should be narrowly focused on whether anyone gets hurt, or there is unfairness. And those who go beyond the first two of care/harm and fairness/cheating in their judgements bring in a whole group of problems. Too much respect for loyalty, authority and purity can lead to jingoism and hostility to outsiders, subjugation of the disadvantaged and racism, homophobia and other forms of oppression. But it is only a small part of the world population who think this way.

21 *The Ecologist*, 'It Can't Be Easy Being George Monbiot', 5 December 2013, http://www.jonathonporritt.com/blog/it-can%E2%80%99t-be-easy-being-george-monbiot.

22 dissident93, 'John Pilger's "Leaked" Emails', 10 August 2011, https://dissident93.wordpress.com/2011/08/10/pilger-leaked-emails/.

23 James Delingpole, 'George Monbiot: The New Christopher Hitchens?', 27 May 2012, http://www.delingpoleworld.com/2012/05/27/george-monbiot-the-new-christopher-hitchens/.

24 J. M. Darley and C. D. Batson (1973). 'From Jerusalem to Jericho: A Study of Situational and Dispositional Variables in Helping Behavior', *Journal of Personality and Social Psychology*, 27, 100–8.

25 Michael I. Norton and Dan Ariely (2011). 'Building a Better America—One Wealth Quintile at a Time', *Perspectives on Psychological Science* 6(9), http://www.people.hbs.edu/mnorton/norton%20ariely.pdf.

26 Bystander effect and social proof are concepts in social psychology that describe how we turn to others to form our own views. Bystanders ignore someone in trouble if they see others doing the same, and social proof, where people emulate the actions of others to reflect correct behaviour, describes why they do so.

27 M. Levine, A. Prosser, D. Evans and S. Reicher (2005). 'Identity and Emergency Intervention: How Social Group Membership and Inclusiveness of Group Boundaries Shapes Helping Behavior', *Personality and Social Psychology Bulletin*, 31, 443–53.

28 Francesca Gino, Shahar Ayal and Dan Ariely (2009). 'Contagion and Differentiation in Unethical Behavior: The Effect of One Bad Apple on the Barrel', *Psychological Science*, 20, 393.

29 Roy F. Baumeister, Laura Smart and Joseph M. Boden (1996). 'Relation of Threatened Egotism to Violence and Aggression: The Dark Side of High Self-esteem', *Psychological Review*, 103(1), 5–33.

30 The anthropologist Scott Atran argues that it is 'sacred values' that are responsible for our most deeply held commitments, and which licence extremes of action such as violence and war.

31 This new judgement was upheld in the House of Lords on the basis that the previous jury had not been properly guided to think about the probability of the consequence before they decided it was foreseeable. Their sentence was accordingly reduced to eight years and they were released in 1989.

32 The Harvard psychologist Fiery Cushman tested the idea that we learn better from outcomes, rather than our intentions, being punished. He had people throw darts at a colour-coded board. The thrower didn't know which colour was high value or low value and was punished for getting it wrong. The dart throwers were divided into two groups: those who nominated the colour they were going for, and those who just threw the dart. The latter group learned to identify the high value colours more effectively.

33 Joshua Knobe (2003). 'Intentional Action and Side Effects in Ordinary Language', *Analysis*, 63, 190–3.

34 But there is a twist. When you do a bad thing out of anger you look overcome with distorting emotion, when you do a good thing out of

compassion you look like your true self. This seems opposite to the Knobe effect.

35 Joshua Greene, *Moral Tribes: Emotion, Reason and the Gap Between Us and Them* (New York, 2013), 70.

36 Paul Bloom, *Against Empathy: The Case for Rational Compassion* (New York, 2016), 9.

37 *Stanford Encyclopedia of Philospohy*, 'Moral Psychology: Empirical Approaches', 19 April 2006, https://plato.stanford.edu/entries/moral-psych-emp/.

38 We should be careful to note a difference between 'act utilitarianism' and 'rule utilitarianism'. Act utilitarianism invites the narrower judgement that an action is morally justified if it in itself brings the greater happiness to the greater number. But the rule version requires that the act accords with a rule which itself brings the greatest happiness to the greatest number.

39 Haidt, *The Righteous Mind*, 71.

40 Ibid., 71.

41 Sandra L. Schneider and James Shanteau (eds), *Emerging Perspectives on Judgment and Decision Research* (Cambridge, 2003), 438–9.

42 Given various combinations of spectators and receivers, Hume concludes that there are four irreducible categories of qualities that exhaustively constitute moral virtue: (1) qualities useful to others, which include benevolence, meekness, charity, justice, fidelity and veracity; (2) qualities useful to oneself, which include industry, perseverance and patience; (3) qualities immediately agreeable to others, which include wit, eloquence and cleanliness and (4) qualities immediately agreeable to oneself, which include good humour, self-esteem and pride. For Hume, most morally significant qualities and actions seem to fall into more than one of these categories.

	Useful	Agreeable
To self	Industry	Pride, self-esteem
To others	Benevolence	Wit, cleanliness

43 Rationality is largely not the basis of moral judgement for us, so if Kant tells us to tell the truth even if it hurts our friends, or Bentham warns us to spend less time with our children so as to benefit the numerous suffering children we have never met, we can appreciate their logic but it still doesn't fit our intuitions.

44 Haidt, *The Righteous Mind*, (London, 2012) 63.

45 Haidt, *The Happiness Hypothesis*, (London, 2006).

Chapter 4

1 Long before I became aware of the books' and the film's colonialist and racist overtones.

2 William Shakespeare, *The Tragedy of King Lear*, Act III. Scene IV, 113–15.

3 The film *Into the Wild* describes well one man's urge to renounce the trappings of civilization for a Thoreau-like adventure of self-reliance.

4 Mark Rowlands, *The Philosopher and the Wolf: Lessons from the Wild on Love, Death and Happiness* (London, 2009), 86.

5 John Tooby, Edge 2017 Question 'Coalitional Psychology', https://www.edge.org/response-detail/27168.

6 Dunbar explains that this is 'the number of people you would not feel embarrassed about joining uninvited for a drink if you happened to bump into them in a bar'.

7 Jonathan Haidt, *The Righteous Mind*, (London, 2012), 76.

8 Clifford Geertz, *The Interpretation of Cultures*, (New York, 1973), 33.

9 Ludwig Wittgenstein, *Philosophical Investigations*, (Oxford, 1998) 223.

10 Stendhal, *Intimate Works*, quoted in Jon Elster, *Sour Grapes: Studies in the Subversion of Reality*, (Cambridge, 1985).

11 Philip Rieff in the *Triumph of the Therapeutic* said Freud democratized genius.

12 John Gottman says in a relationship you need five positive interactions to compensate for one negative one.

13 A thinly veiled depiction of Roth himself, who appears in several of his novels.

14 I'll note here that a Jordanian–Irish person writing about a Jewish novelist portraying a black man pretending to be white is layered with partial comprehension and the potential for unintended insensitivities of its own. This in itself bears on the themes I want to highlight in this book.

15 Chimimanda Adichie in her novel *Americanah* features hair repeatedly as a marker that can force black people to the margins.

16 Friedrich Nietzsche, (New York, 1974) [1882] *The Gay Science*, 310.

17 This is where humans take on animal form and become dissolved in their worlds like the cows on page 51. Between pages 47 and 52 we're given viscerally apt writing, like Hardy's Tess of the D'Urbervilles walking through the milking fields looking for the spoiling garlic, dragging thistle milk and slug slime in her wake.

Chapter 5

1 Emine Saner, 'Mitch Winehouse on Amy the Film', *The Guardian* (1 May 2015), www.theguardian.com/music/2015/may/01/mitch-winehouse-interview-amy-documentary-film.

2 Dan P. McAdams, *The Art and Science of Personality Development* (Guildford, 2015).

3 These sketches of Trump come from McAdams's piece in the *Atlantic*, summarized in the *Guardian* article from which these quotations

are taken (Dan P. McAdams, 'A Psychological Trap: Making Sense of Donald Trump's Life and Personality', *The Guardian* (5 August 2016), www.theguardian.com/us-news/2016/aug/05/donald-trump-psychology-personality-republicans-election).

4 You can see how this plays out when you contrast the formative stories of the WEIRD liberals discussed in Chapter 3 with those of a more conservative bent:

When asked to describe in detail the most important episodes in their self-defining life narratives, conservatives told stories in which authorities enforce strict rules and protagonists learn the value of self-discipline and personal responsibility, whereas liberals recalled autobiographical scenes in which main characters develop empathy and learn to open themselves up to new people and foreign perspectives. When asked to account for the development of their own religious faith and moral beliefs, conservatives underscored deep feelings about respect for authority, allegiance to one's group, and purity of the self, whereas liberals emphasized their deep feelings regarding human suffering and social fairness.

D.P.M. McAdams et al. (2008), 'Family Metaphors and Moral Intuitions: How Conservatives and Liberals Narrate Their Lives', *Journal of Personality and Social Psychology* (95), 978.

5 Christopher Booker, *The Seven Basic Plots: Why We Tell Stories* (London, 2004). He goes rather farther than his remit, it seems to me, when criticizing great works for failing to match the basic plots well enough.

6 Even though he calls the book *The Seven Basic Plots* and these form the structure of the first section of the book, later on he adds two more. The first is 'Rebellion Against "The One"', where the protagonist resists a tremendous enemy force until overwhelmed by that power. The second is 'Mystery', where someone steps into an awful but unexplained event and has to make sense of what happened.

7 Alasdair MacIntyre, *After Virtue: A Study in Moral Theory* (London, 1985).

8 Wittgenstein, *The Brown Book* (Oxford, 1958), 87.

9 Some, of course, are written by the deceased themselves. An obituary editor says you can always tell when an obit was written by the person themselves because the penultimate paragraph tends to go 'one area of their many achievements that was overlooked'.

10 Though it is telling that Spike Milligan's 'See, I told you I was ill' is rendered in Gaelic so as to come across as less blunt to passing onlookers. We don't think of death a laughing matter. Presumably Irish speakers are considered to be more philosophically resilient.

11 James Wood, *The Nearest Thing to Life* (London, 2015), 19.

12 Alexander Nehamas, *On Friendship* (New York, 2016), 125.

13 This idea was suggested to me by the writer and technology theorist Tom Chatfield.

14 Julian Baggini, *The Ego Trick: What Does It Mean To Be You?* (London, 2012).

15 William Shakespeare, *Macbeth*, Act V. Scene V, lines 24–28.

16 James Wood, *The Nearest Thing to Life* (London, 2015), 53.

Index